CULTURE SMART!
SOUTH AFRICA

Isabella Morris

·K·U·P·E·R·A·R·D·

ISBN 978 1 85733 872 0

British Library Cataloguing in Publication Data
A CIP catalogue entry for this book is available from the
British Library

First published in Great Britain
by Kuperard, an imprint of Bravo Ltd
59 Hutton Grove, London N12 8DS
Tel: +44 (0) 20 8446 2440   Fax: +44 (0) 20 8446 2441
www.culturesmart.co.uk
Inquiries: sales@kuperard.co.uk

Series Editor Geoffrey Chesler
Design Bobby Birchall

Printed in Malaysia

About the Author

ISABELLA MORRIS is an award-winning South African writer and journalist. After graduating from the University of the Witwatersrand with an M.A. in Creative Writing, she traveled extensively in Asia and Africa and contributed feature and travel articles to mainstream South African newspapers. During South Africa's 2016 municipal elections she was campaign chief-of-staff to the current executive mayor of Johannesburg. Today Isabella is a writer and editor, and teaches travel writing, non-fiction, fiction, and short-story writing workshops. She lives in Johannesburg with her husband.

contents

contents

Map of South Africa

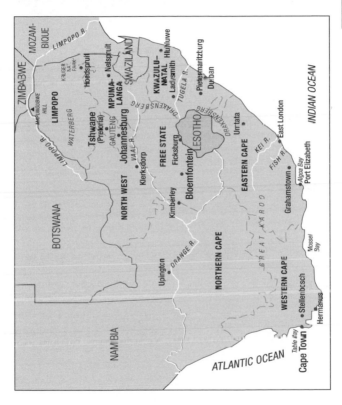

introduction

"How do I live in this strange place?"
Bernoldus Niemand (alter ego of James Phillips, rock singer)

If South Africa had a DNA test, the diversity of the world would be found in its genetic coding. Since the first *Australopithecus* inhabited the region 2.5 million years ago, South Africa has been home to different groups moving across the landscape, and today is still home to people from across the globe, settling on its shores for economic, political, and social reasons, attracted as ever by the country's bounty.

South Africa has eleven official languages, nine major black tribes, two major white groups, Asians, and Coloureds (the official designation for mixed-race people). It embraces all religions, has communists in its parliament, yet is a free market economy. There are the very rich and the very poor. Women sit in the cabinet, yet rural women are the least likely to have an education. So how indeed does one "live in this strange place"?

It is impossible to generalize about a people as diverse as the South Africans. They're not all good, and they're not all bad. What they are is a nation of hope, where the majority want a future that seeks to embody what the writer Olive Schreiner called a "great, healthy, harmonious, and desirable nation."

In spite of all the goodwill, South Africa has many problems, such as crime and HIV/AIDS, and in some instances the apparent loss of old values in favor of the new. Many traditions are being eroded by assimilation, languages such as Afrikaans are changing, and Kasi (a township language) is the lingua franca of black youth, many of whom no longer speak their native languages.

South Africa is an in-between land. It stands on the cusp of the old and the new, the First and the Third Worlds, the North and the South. This book will introduce you to a vibrant society in transition. It examines the often painful past to explain some of the complexities and contradictions of modern South African society. It looks at how people relate to each other, at home, work, and play, and offers advice on what to expect and how to behave in different situations. South Africans are big-hearted and optimistic. Make the effort to understand them, and they will welcome you unreservedly.

South Africa has been variously described as "a country with a heartbeat as strong as a jackhammer," "God's armpit," "an intellectual *dorp* (village)," and a "pioneering nation," but political commentator Rian Malan probably puts it best: "This is South Africa, where nothing can be taken for granted, even if you see it with your own eyes."

Key Facts

Official Name	The Republic of South Africa	
Capital Cities	Tshwane (formerly Pretoria), administrative capital; Cape Town, legislative capital; Bloemfontein, judicial capital	
Cities of the Major Metropolitan Municipalities (population estimates based on 2011 figures)	Buffalo City (East London, pop. 478,600); City of Cape Town (pop. 3.4m); City of Johannesburg (pop. incl. Soweto 3.7m); City of Tshwane (Pretoria pop. 1.6m); Ekurhuleni (East Rand, pop. 3.2m); eThekwini (Durban, pop. 3.4m); Mangaung (Bloemfontein, pop. 747,400); Nelson Mandela Bay (Port Elizabeth, pop. 967,600)	
Area	470,693 square miles (1,219,090 sq. km)	
Climate	Semidesert to subtropical, but largely moderate. The southwestern Cape has a Mediterranean-type climate.	
Population	55,908 900 (2016)	
Ethnic Makeup	Black 45,109,900; Coloured 4,897,200; White 4,515,800; Indian/Asian 1,386,000	
Language	There are 11 official languages. While Afrikaans is the most widely spoken, English is the dominant commercial language.	Language speakers as % of total (2011): Afrikaans 13.5%; English 9.6%; isiNdebele 2.1%; isiXhosa 16%; isiZulu 22.7%; Sepedi 9.1%; Sesotho 7.6%; Setswana 8%; SiSwati 2.5%; Tshivenda 2.4%; Xitsonga 4.5%; Other 2%
Age Structure	0–14 years 15–24 years 25–54 years	28.34% 18.07% 41.44%

Religion	Zion Christian 11.1%; Pentecostal/ Charismatic 8.2%; Roman Catholic 7.1%; Methodist 6.8%; Dutch Reformed 6.7% Anglican 3.8%; Other Christian 36%; Islam 1.5%; Hinduism 1.2%; Native beliefs 0.3%; Judaism 0.2%; no religion 15.1% (2001 census)	
Government	Constitutional democracy. Bicameral parliament consisting of the National Assembly (the lower house) and the National Council of Provinces (the upper house)	
Currency	South African Rand (ZAR)	1 rand = 100 cents
Media	State-owned TV and radio channels, two independent national TV channels, several independent local channels, many state and independent radio channels, many state-influenced newspapers, and very few independent newspapers. Many of the media outlets use English as their language of communication.	
Electricity	220/230 volts, 50 Hz	Plugs generally 15-amp 3-prong, or 5-amp 2-prong with round pins. US appliances may require a transformer.
TV/Video	PAL I system	
Telephone	South Africa's country code is 27.	Dial out 09. Three-digit code must be dialed when calling locally. Four cell phone networks
Internet Domain	.za	
Time	GMT + 2 hours	

chapter one

LAND &
PEOPLE

GEOGRAPHICAL OVERVIEW

Located at the southern tip of the African continent,
South Africa is the twenty-fifth-largest country in the
world. Probably its most notable geographical feature
is the 1,739-mile (2,800-km) coastline, which stretches
from the border with Namibia on the icy Atlantic west
coast to Mozambique on the warm Indian Ocean east
coast. Its northern neighbors are Namibia, Botswana,
and Zimbabwe; Mozambique and Swaziland lie to the
east, and it completely surrounds Lesotho. The Prince
Edward and Marion Islands in the sub-Antarctic Indian

Ocean were annexed in
1947, and are 1,193 miles
(1,920 km) southeast of
Cape Town.

The terrain is
dominated by a high
(4,000–6,000 ft. /1,220–
1,830 m) central plateau
of rolling grassland
known as the Highveld.
On the south, east, and
west, it is ringed by the
Great Escarpment, an
almost continuous ridge
of mountain ranges,

which, in turn, give way to coastal lowlands. South Africa has been referred to as a "world in one country" due to the geographical diversity of its different climatic regions.

CLIMATE

The climate is generally classified as semi-arid, but there are many microclimates. The Mediterranean climate of the southwestern Cape has wet winters and dry, hot summers, and the characteristic South Easter/North Wester that blows intermittently throughout the year. The southeastern Cape coast, commonly referred to as the Garden Route, is lush and green, with one of the richest bio-diverse ecosystems in the world. Further north up the coast is the subtropical landscape of Kwa-Zulu Natal (KZN), where sugarcane fields stretch as far as the eye can see.

Inland, rocky hills and mountains rise from the Karoo plateau's scrubland. This semi-desert region is an area of extremes, with dry, hot summers and icy cold winters. The eastern Karoo yields to the Free State's semi-arid, flat landscape, which has a somewhat higher rainfall. The Highveld is situated north of the Vaal River and its altitude—Johannesburg is a mile (1,740 m) above sea level—ensures mild winters and balmy summers. Toward the northern border with Botswana and Zimbabwe and east of the Drakensberg Mountains, the inland plateau gives way to lowlands known as the Lowveld; here temperatures rise, especially in the bushveld (subtropical woodland areas). It is hottest in the deep interior.

Those looking to cool down or for a place to ski in winter head for the Drakensberg slopes on the eastern escarpment above the KZN midlands.

ETHNIC GROUPS

The diversity of ethnic groups in South Africa makes it virtually impossible to characterize a typical South African. While official sources categorize blacks, whites, Coloureds (mixed-race), and Asians, this doesn't take into account the complex makeup of each group. The largest group, black South Africans, can be further broken down into the traditional Zulu, Xhosa, Sotho, Tswana, Tsonga, Venda, Pedi, Shangaan, and Swazi-speaking people, but this ignores the significant number of black people from across the continent who have made their home in South Africa, especially Zimbabweans and Mozambicans, but also Rwandans, Congolese, Malawians, Nigerians, Ghanaians, Ethiopians, and Somalis.

The Asians no longer just consist of the historical Indian population and the relatively small South African Chinese population—both originally indentured laborers. It now includes a significant number of Chinese from the Republic of China, who are largely "economically sponsored" migrants, part of China's "go out into the world" policy. Bangladeshi and Pakistani migrants have also settled in South Africa in recent years, some arriving as skilled workers (usually in IT) and then entering South Africa's informal sector and becoming traders.

Whites comprise the traditional English- and Afrikaans-speaking populations, and now European contract workers who have settled in South Africa as multinational companies have invested in the country.

So South Africans today are very diverse, and while migrants may still gravitate to the areas in which their compatriots have settled, on any commercial street you'll find people from all over the world.

The first to arrive were the majority Bantu-speaking peoples, who reached the northwestern parts of the country in the early centuries of the common era. Dutch and English settlers dominated the colonial era (1652–1910), but during the apartheid period (1948–94) skilled immigrants from Europe were encouraged. Coalminers from Wales and Scotland were drawn to the gold and diamond mines, where racial job segregation meant they were employed as managers and in skilled positions.

There have always been social and economic disparities between the peoples of South Africa. The privileged position that white South Africans have enjoyed since colonial times persists and is the source of much frustration for blacks. On the other hand, decades into democracy, many young whites are not willing to accept the guilt of apartheid and regard the stringent Black Economic Empowerment laws (see pages 149–50) as a bar to personal progress. As a result of what they consider to be discriminatory economic policies, many have become economic emigrants. Generally, however, South Africans don't dwell on the negative, and have an optimistic outlook.

A BRIEF HISTORY
Prehistoric Times

South Africa's history goes back to the dawn of humankind. The first *Australopithecus* inhabited the region at least 2.5 million years ago, and there is evidence that the first modern humans lived in the Klasies River Caves in the Eastern Cape during the Middle Stone Age, 125,000 years ago. This DNA group is still prevalent in the indigenous Khoi and San people of South Africa.

The Hofmeyr Skull, found in 1952 in the Eastern Cape Province, dates back 36,000 years and is similar to Eurasian skulls of the same age, confirming the

"Out of Africa" hypothesis—that modern humans migrated from their place of origin in sub-Saharan Africa about 40,000 years ago and populated the world. The latest find, in 2015, at the world-renowned Cradle of Mankind world heritage site is the *Homo naledi*, a previously unknown species of *Homo*.

Pre-Colonial Period

Around three and a half thousand years BCE proto-Bantu-speaking peoples started to expand across the African continent from the region of Cameroon and Nigeria. By 1500 BCE Bantu-speakers had reached the great Central African rain forest, and by 500 BCE they had emerged on to the savannahs in Angola and Zambia. In around 300 CE, groups reached the coastal areas of modern-day KwaZulu Natal (KZN), and by 500 CE present-day Northern Province. The Bantu were herdsmen and iron-using agriculturalists. In South Africa they encountered the indigenous Neolithic hunting and foraging peoples, the Khoi and the San.

In the fourth or fifth century the Bantu settled in the area south of the Limpopo River and conquered, absorbed, or displaced the Khoi and San, driving them out to the drier semidesert areas. They moved south, and the earliest iron works found in modern-day KZN date to around 1050 CE. The Nguni group of Bantu-speakers—consisting of the Zulu, Xhosa, Swazi, and Ndebele tribes—settled on the eastern coast of present-day South Africa. The Tswana, Pedi, and Sotho settled in the Highveld, and the Venda, Lemba, Shangaan, and Tsonga settled in the northeast of the country. There is linguistic proof of assimilation between Bantu-speakers and the Khoi and San, and this is particularly noticeable in the Xhosa and Zulu languages, which feature the characteristic Khoi San click consonants.

Colonial Period

The Portuguese mariner Bartolomeu Dias was the
first European to round the Cape, in 1488, during his
expedition to discover a trade route to the Far East.
He named the rocky tip of the Cape Peninsula the
Cape of Storms. Eleven years later, his compatriot
Vasco da Gama passed the Great Fish River on the east
coast of South Africa where Dias had turned back. Da
Gama named that part of the east coast Natal, pressed
northward to Zanzibar, and successfully reached India,
opening up the trade route to the East via the Cape.

It was only in the 1600s that the Dutch East India
Company (Vereenigde Oost-Indische Compagnie,
or VOC) decided to take a closer look at the Cape of
Storms, as they required a base camp for their sailors
traveling the spice route to the East, where ships could
be repaired and fresh supplies taken on board. In 1652,
the VOC sent a small expedition commanded by Jan
van Riebeeck to establish a settlement at the newly
named Cape of Good Hope. The indigenous Khoi were
nomadic herdsmen, not agriculturalists, so the Dutch
established market gardens to feed the passing crews.
At first Company servants were not allowed to trade
independently, but Van Riebeeck gained permission to
free them from
their contracts,
and these "free
burghers" began
to trade, farm, and
help with defense.
The supply
station gradually
became a settler
community, and
other people from

the Netherlands and Northern Europe, including Huguenots from France, were attracted to the colony in the Cape. These people were the forebears of the Afrikaner South Africans.

Some settlers moved inland and many became nomadic livestock farmers (Trekboers) who continued to expand north and east, competing with the Khoi for the best grazing lands. Self-contained, pious, and isolated, they lived completely independent of official control.

The Khoi population was largely expelled, and their numbers were further reduced by outbreaks of

smallpox. To supply the growing need for labor, the VOC imported slaves from other colonies in the East Indies, and the descendants of these slaves became known as the Cape Malays. Many interracial unions resulted in the creation of the Cape Coloured population. The first governor of the Dutch colony, Simon van der Stel, was himself of mixed-race origin.

When the pro-French Batavian Republic was proclaimed in the Netherlands in 1795, Britain was desperate to keep the colony out of French hands and seized the Cape, but returned it to the Dutch in 1803. However, in 1806, during the Napoleonic Wars, Britain again wrested control of the Cape from the Netherlands. The Dutch settlers balked at British attempts to anglicize them and began to move inland, away from the British administration. As they moved eastward up the coast they encountered the southernmost Bantu tribe, the Xhosa, who were already established in the area and herded cattle in the region of the Great Fish River.

Britain was only interested in the Cape as a strategic port, and in 1815 paid the Netherlands six million pounds for the colony. To swell British numbers in the colony and increase their influence, about 5,000 British immigrants were settled in Grahamstown and Port Elizabeth in 1820.

Soon, competition for land led to conflict on the eastern Cape frontier—between the Bantu tribes, between the Xhosa and the European settlers, and between the British and the Boers, as the Dutch-speaking settlers came to be known. The Xhosa or Cape Frontier wars, which began under the Dutch and ended under the British, lasted from 1779 to 1879.

The Great Trek (1835–46)
The abolition of slavery throughout the British Empire in 1834 caused the conservative Calvinist Dutch settlers great offense, compounded by the amount of compensation offered and the fact that claims had to be lodged in Britain. Exasperated by British interference and liberalism, and disillusioned with Britain's policy toward the conflict with the Xhosa on the eastern frontier, they concluded that emigration was the only way to secure their economic, political, and cultural future.

So it was that between 1835 and 1846 thousands of Boers trekked into the interior of southern Africa. The collective determination and courage shown during this great movement laid the foundation of Afrikaner nationalism. While many consider the move into the interior to have been a God-fearing, peaceful process, the Great Trek would cause immense upheaval.

During their reconnaissance expeditions, the Voortrekkers (pioneers) were advised that Natal south of the Tugela River and the central Highveld region on either side of the Vaal River were suitable for settlement and largely uninhabited. This was due to the interior having been ravaged by the *Mfecane*.

The *Mfecane* (c. 1815–40)

The *Mfecane* ("crushing" in Zulu) refers to a period of chaos and warfare between indigenous chiefdoms and clans in southern Africa. The expansion of the

militaristic Zulu kingdom under King Shaka caused waves of disruption and warfare to reach other areas. It led certain tribes to dominate in some territories and others to consolidate in groups elsewhere. When Shaka's lieutenant, Mzilikazi, fell out with him, he went on to conquer the Transvaal, and almost depopulated the region with widespread killing and devastation. The dead are estimated at between a million and two million people. Some tribes moved to other areas, but were soon ousted by the incoming Boers.

In their quest for independence, the Boers, too, caused enormous disruption in the South African interior. Hundreds of thousands were affected. During Boer onslaughts against local tribes in the northern and eastern Transvaal, thousands of children were captured and used as indentured labor until adulthood. Mzilikazi confronted the Boers and was humiliatingly defeated at Vegkop, then again at Mosega, and finally besieged in the Marico Valley. He was forced to flee across the Limpopo River into present-day Zimbabwe in 1838.

The Boer Republics

On December 16, 1838, in present-day KZN, 470 Trekboers led by Andries Pretorius defeated 15,000 to 20,000 Zulu attackers on the banks of the Ncome River, in a victory known as the Battle of Blood River. Two months later the Zulu King Dingane was overthrown by his half-brother Prince Mpande at the Battle of Maquongqe. In 1838 the Boers declared the short-lived Republic of Natalia, with Pretorius as President. Britain, however, refused to recognize their independence and in 1842 occupied Port Natal. The Boers resisted but were finally defeated.

Elsewhere in the interior the Boers seized land from several local chiefs and either took over their crops or uprooted them. Land was not "owned" in African societies in the modern sense of the word, but the Boers often "persuaded" African chiefs to "sell" land to them— communal land that they never really owned or had rights over. Nevertheless, large tracts of land were sold very cheaply, often for just a few cattle.

In 1852 and 1854 the Boers established the Vaal and Orange River Republics respectively. In 1877 Britain annexed the South African Republic (the Vaal Republic), using a special warrant. The Transvaal Boers led by Paul Kruger objected but, as the Zulu threat remained, acquiesced, though greatly resenting the British occupation. Zulu dominance in the region ended with the defeat of the Zulu King Cetshwayo, son of Mpande, in the Anglo–Zulu War of 1879.

Free now to act, the Transvaal Boers declared independence from the British Empire, and the First Anglo–Boer War broke out on December 16, 1880. The Boers' use of unconventional guerrilla tactics, involving mobility, marksmanship, and high use of defensive positions, proved vastly superior, and the result was decisive defeat for the British. The Pretoria convention of 1881 ceded the second independence of the South African Republic under British sovereignty, with British control of foreign relations.

Diamonds and Gold
The discovery of the world's richest diamond deposits near Kimberley in 1867 and of gold in the Witwatersrand area of the SAR in 1886 reignited imperial interest. The agrarian economy shifted toward industrialization, allied to the development of mining, and South Africa's first industrial city, Johannesburg,

was born. Gold made the Transvaal the richest state in southern Africa and, for the Colonial Office, raised the specter of a confederation of Boer republics that could threaten the Royal Navy base at Simon's Town on the Cape Peninsula.

European fortune hunters now flocked to the new republics, potentially exceeding the number of Boers. In time, individual prospectors formed partnerships and alliances that would give rise to the corporate giants of today. Capital investment in technology and the huge demand for migrant African labor—housed in closed compounds—created a social and industrial revolution. Britain, in need of gold to underpin sterling, now viewed the archaic, inefficient Boer republics as an obstacle to development and to its imperial ambitions. The question of who would control the lucrative Witwatersrand gold mines came to a head in the Second Anglo–Boer War.

The South African War (Second Anglo–Boer War, 1899–1902)

The Colonial Secretary Joseph Chamberlain used the issue of the rights of the *uitlanders* (foreign residents) within the SAR in an attempt to incorporate the Transvaal and the Orange Free State into a federation under British control. His political maneuverings were countered by an ultimatum by President Kruger, on October 9, 1899, giving the British government forty-eight hours to withdraw all troops from the borders of the two Boer republics. Britain rejected the ultimatum, and the South African Republic and Orange Free State declared war on the biggest empire in the world.

British forces quickly seized control of the Free State and Transvaal, which were officially annexed in 1900. However, the Boers refused to surrender and reverted to

guerrilla warfare, blending into the farmlands, which provided hiding places, supplies, and horses. The British retaliated with a scorched earth policy—burning farms, slaughtering livestock— and set up concentration camps where civilian farmers, women, and children were incarcerated. Many prisoners, especially children, died of disease.

Black farmers were held in separate camps. A network of blockhouses, strong points, and barbed-wire fences partitioned off the conquered territory. Mounted infantry units systematically tracked down the highly mobile Boer guerrillas. This war of attrition finally forced the Boers to surrender.

Inevitably, black Africans were caught up in the conflict. Although the policy on both sides was to minimize the role of non-whites, the need for manpower meant that in the end about 10,000 black men were attached to Boer units, where a handful unofficially fought in combat. The British Army employed Africans as wagon drivers, spies, and guides, and eventually as soldiers. By 1902 there were about 30,000 armed Africans in the British Army.

The war ended with the Treaty of Vereeniging in May 1902, on terms that were surprisingly lenient. Among other concessions, a key clause assured the Boers that blacks would not be given the vote before the restoration of self-government. The Boer leaders now gave full support to the new political system. Together with the

Cape Colony and the Natal Colony, the former republics were incorporated into the Union of South Africa in 1910, which the Boers came to control, despite the drive by Alfred, Lord Milner, the British High Commissioner, to anglicize the Transvaal.

The South Africa Act of 1909, which became the constitution of the Union, established English and Dutch as the official languages of South Africa, with equal status under the law, and required all government documents and parliamentary proceedings to be published in both languages. Today, English remains one of the official languages of the Republic of South Africa. Dutch was extended to include its local variant, Afrikaans, in 1925, and was replaced by Afrikaans in the constitution of 1961. In 1934 South Africa became a self-governing dominion within the British Empire.

A "White Man's Country"

The South Africa Act did little to protect the rights of black Africans, and laid the foundations for the later establishment of apartheid.

The relatively liberal Cape Colony had a system of non-racial franchise, in which the voting qualifications of education and wealth applied equally to all males, regardless of race. The Act permitted the Cape Province to keep a restricted version of its franchise. Thus the Cape became the only province in the new South Africa where Coloureds and black Africans could vote; however, the Union parliament was given the power to overrule the Cape's electoral system by a two-thirds vote, and over the years legislation was passed that slowly eroded its color-blind voters' register.

Among other segregationist laws, the Union parliament enacted the 1913 Natives' Land Act, which earmarked 8 percent of South Africa's available land for black occupancy. White people, who constituted 20 percent of the population, held 90 percent of the land. The Land Act would form a cornerstone of legalized racial discrimination for the next nine decades.

Black Resistance and the ANC
The country's educated African elite regarded Britain as the guarantor of equal rights. Appalled by the unfolding betrayal of their hopes, they organized a South African Native Convention in Bloemfontein in March 1909 to protest, respectfully, against the racist provisions of the proposed South Africa Act. A mission to lobby Parliament in London, led by William Schreiner, a former Prime Minister of the Cape Colony, followed to no avail. South Africa's blacks had been sold out.

African leaders now convened a historic conference in Bloemfontein on January 9, 1912, at which Pixley Seme, a young attorney, launched the South African Native National Congress, the forerunner of the African

National Congress (ANC). The event went unreported
by the white press.

Moderate and constitutional, the SANNC
campaigned against the infamous Land Act of 1913,
which forced many non-whites from their farms into the
cities and towns to work, and restricted their movement
within the country. By 1919, it was leading a campaign
against the compulsory ID passes for non-whites. In
the mid-1920s black people were also represented by
the radical Industrial and Commercial Union and the
previously whites-only Communist Party. In 1923, the
SANNC became the African National Congress, and
in 1929 the ANC supported a militant mineworkers'
strike. By the mid-1940s the ANC had become a mass
movement and leader in the struggle against white
domination.

The Apartheid Years
Founded in 1915 by Afrikaner nationalists, the National
Party (NP) was in government from 1948 until 1994. Its
policies formalized and extended the existing system of
racial discrimination into the legal system of *apartheid*
(or "separate development")—the political, economic,
and social separation of the races in order to maintain
the white minority's control of South Africa. Other goals
were the establishment of an independent republic,
and the promotion of Afrikaner culture. In 1959 the
NP government created the so-called "Homelands" (or
"Bantustans") for ten black tribes. The aim was to move
all black South Africans into one of these homelands
(although they could continue to work in South Africa
as "guest workers"), leaving the rest of the country
with a white majority. As the homelands were seen as
embryonic independent nations, black South Africans
were registered as citizens of the homelands, not of the

country as a whole, and only had political rights in them. Thus the three token parliamentary seats reserved for white representatives of black South Africans in the Cape Province were scrapped.

Coloureds were removed from the Common Roll of the Cape Province in 1953. Instead of voting for the same representatives as whites, they could now only vote for four white representatives to speak for them. Later, in 1968, they were disenfranchised altogether. This made the electorate entirely white, as Asians had never had any representation.

The former German colony of South West Africa (now Namibia), which South Africa had occupied in the First World War, was effectively annexed as a fifth province, with seven members elected to represent its pro-Nationalist white citizens in Parliament. These measures all bolstered the NP parliamentary majority.

Apartheid laws passed after 1948 included the notorious Prohibition of Mixed Marriages Act,

the Immorality Act, the Population Registration Act, and the Group Areas Act, which prohibited non-white males from being in certain areas of the country (especially at night) unless they were employed there. The consequences of these laws were often devastating and had a profound social and psychological impact.

After holding a referendum, white South Africa declared itself a republic, formally ending its constitutional ties with the United Kingdom on May 31, 1961. This move was accompanied by South Africa's expulsion from the British Commonwealth. The

Afrikaner republican dream had become a reality, and the government set about eliminating residual British influence.

The Freedom Struggle

The ANC responded to the assault on human rights with non-violent action, calling for strikes, boycotts, and civil defiance. The Defiance Campaign in the 1950s was a multiracial political movement of mass resistance. The government countered by banning leaders and enacting new laws to stop the activity.

In 1955 a Congress of the People drafted and adopted the Freedom Charter, stating the core principles and aspirations of the South African Congress Alliance—the African National Congress and its allies the South African Communist Party, the South African Indian Congress, the South African Congress of Democrats, and the Coloured People's Congress. The government claimed that this was a communist document, and the leaders of the ANC and Congress were later arrested and tried for treason.

In 1960 a group of between 5,000 and 10,000 people converged on the local police station in the township of Sharpeville, offering themselves up for arrest for not carrying their passbooks. Sixty-nine were killed when police opened fire on the protesters.

In 1961, partly in response to the Sharpeville massacre, Umkhonto we Sizwe (shortened to MK), meaning "Spear of the Nation," was established as the military wing of the ANC. It was designated a terrorist group by the South African government, and later classified as such by the United States. With political and military support from the Soviet Union, MK began the armed struggle

against apartheid with acts of sabotage aimed at state installations, and in the early stages was reluctant to target civilians.

The Soweto Uprising

In June 1976 about 20,000 black students from many schools in Soweto (South Western Townships, outside Johannesburg) held protest demonstrations against the introduction of Afrikaans, "the language of the oppressor," as the medium of instruction in local schools. They were met with police brutality and hundreds were killed. As the clashes continued the Rand devalued and the government was plunged into a crisis. The ANC distributed leaflets linking the issue to its revolutionary program. Images of the riots spread around the world and brought international condemnation on the government. The UN General Assembly had already suspended South Africa from the organization in 1974. Now the Security Council passed Resolution 392, which strongly condemned the incident and the apartheid government. ANC exiles called for international action and economic sanctions against South Africa.

Following Soweto, the police and army were given a free hand in "high-risk" areas. In November 1977 the Security Council imposed a mandatory arms embargo on South Africa. The government's response was to further militarize the country and establish its own arms manufacturing industry. In the mid-1980s, police and army death squads conducted state-sponsored assassinations of dissidents and activists both within the country and in neighboring states.

The South African Border War (1966–90)

This war, fought between the South African Defence Force and the People's Liberation Army of Namibia,

was closely linked to the Angolan Civil War. The South African government contained the conflict to areas outside the country's borders, but it had a great impact on South African politics and social life. Government propaganda painted it as a war against Soviet expansion. Life on the home front was was infused with anti-communist sentiment, and there was forced conscription to feed the war machine.

Several factors combined to bring the Border War to an end. It was a drain on South Africa's coffers and the white public grew war-weary. There was the additional wave of civic unrest among black South Africans that threatened internal stability. Cuba's President Castro was also under pressure to withdraw from an open-ended guerrilla war in Southern Africa, and South Africa had acquired a nuclear weapons capability. In 1988, Cuba and South Africa agreed a mutual withdrawal of troops from Angola. On the back of this protracted war, and increasing unrest among South African blacks, President F. W. de Klerk realized that South Africans needed to sit down and negotiate an inclusive future.

The Beginning of the End

The dissolution of the Soviet Union in the late 1980s meant the ANC could no longer depend on Soviet support. It also meant the South African government could no longer link apartheid to the protection of Christian values and civilization in the face of the "red menace." Both sides were forced to the negotiating table. Confronted by mounting local and international opposition, President de Klerk took the plunge. He unbanned all political parties and on February 2, 1990, . released the ANC's iconic leader Nelson Mandela from Robben Island, where he had been incarcerated for twenty-seven years.

De Klerk entered into negotiations with the liberation movements to transform South Africa into a

democratic country, with the result that in June 1991 all apartheid laws were finally rescinded, opening the way for elections three years later. In a referendum held on March 17, 1992, the white electorate voted 68 percent in favor of democracy. De Klerk and Mandela jointly won the

Nobel Peace Prize in 1993 for their role in the ending of apartheid.

Over the years, resistance to Afrikaner nationalism had not been confined exclusively to people of color or the ANC. Anti-apartheid organizations included anti-fascist Second World War veterans, white liberals, pacifists, communists, the Pan African Congress, the Black Consciousness Movement, and the non-racial United Democratic Front, a coalition of civic, church, student, trade union, and other bodies. However, the non-racial ANC represented the main opposition and played a crucial role in resolving the conflict through the peacemaking and peace-building processes.

The New South Africa
On April 27, 1994, after decades of armed struggle and international political activism, the ANC won an overwhelming victory in South Africa's first multiracial elections, thus ending a regime that had dehumanized the majority of South Africans for decades. Nelson Mandela became the first black state president and remained in office until 1999. The outcome gave rise

to a remarkable feeling of fellowship between all South Africans and a strong desire to build a new, inclusive, South African society.

The ANC has dominated national politics since then, in an increasingly uncomfortable alliance with the South African Communist Party and the Congress of South African Trade Unions. Its historic role in the freedom struggle earned it the gratitude and loyalty of the electorate, but its performance in government has fallen far short of the vision of its founding fathers.

The district, metropolitan, and local municipal elections of 2016 saw the ANC lose its majority in the major metropolises. The opposition Democratic Alliance, already controlling the Cape Province and Cape Town, with the support of other minority parties took charge of key municipalities such as Johannesburg, Tshwane, and Midvaal in Gauteng Province and Nelson Mandela Bay in the Eastern Cape. Although the ANC government had initiated ambitious programs to deliver housing, schools, and clinics, corruption and mismanagement have impeded their delivery. The new DA authorities pledged to kick-start service delivery, clean up corruption, and restore an ailing and mismanaged economy.

Anger at the slow redress of social inequality produced another result in the emergence of a minority black opposition in the form of the Economic Freedom Fighters, whose members split from the ANC, and who have gained popularity among those who feel disadvantaged. This party promotes black nationalism and radical land reform. Its support has remained at roughly 10 percent—not enough to win power, but enough to make them a force to be reckoned with in forming alliances to keep the ANC in check.

GOVERNMENT

The Republic of South Africa is a constitutional democracy with a three-tier system of government that is subject to the Constitution. The new post-apartheid Constitution was drawn up after the 1994 elections and came into force in 1997. It includes an extensive Bill of Rights and is considered one of the most progressive constitutions in the world.

The Constitution enshrines a system of cooperative governance: it contains a set of principles that require the national, provincial, and local organs of government to cooperate in good faith and to act in the best interests of the people, in a democratic and free South Africa.

The Executive

The seat of government is in Pretoria. The executive is led by the state president, who is elected by the majority party and currently serves for no more than two five-year terms. The cabinet consists of ministers who are appointed by the president. There are nine provincial executive councils, each headed by its own premier.

The Legislature

Parliament sits in Cape Town. It consists of the National Assembly, with 350–400 members, and the National Council of Provinces, with 90 delegates.

The National Assembly is elected through a system of proportional representation for a term of five years. It elects the President, provides a national forum for the public consideration of issues, passes legislation, and scrutinizes and oversees executive actions.

The NCOP is made up of ten representatives from each province, elected for a period of five years, fifty-four permanent members, and thirty-six special delegates. It represents provincial interests in the national government, which requires a mandate from

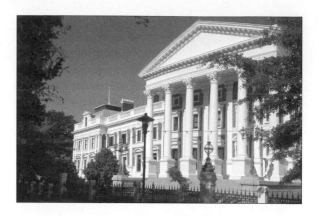

the provinces before it can make certain decisions. It is the link between parliament and the provincial and local government legislatures.

The Judiciary
Roman–Dutch law is the common law in South Africa. The Constitution is the supreme law of the land. Most lower-level legal activity occurs at a magistrates' court level, then at a high court, an appellate division, and the constitutional court at the highest level. The judiciary is headed by a chief justice. Judges are appointed by the president in consultation with the Judicial Service Commission.

The "Chapter Nine" institutions are a group of organizations established by the Constitution to strengthen and defend democracy. They include the Office of the Public Protector, the Human Rights Commission, the Commission for the Promotion and Protection of the Rights of Cultural, Religious, and Linguistic Communities, the Commission for Gender Equality, the Auditor General, and the Independent Communications Authority in South Africa.

TRANSITIONS

When Nelson Mandela died at the age of ninety-five in December 2013 there was an outpouring of tributes around the world. His funeral, attended by about ninety representatives of foreign states, including Presidents Obama and Raul Castro, was an event of international importance. His quiet dignity, humanity, and rejection of bitterness had ensured that the country held together during the transition to majority rule. His moral authority gave the world an inspiring example of principled leadership, and set the bar high for future South African presidents.

At the dawn of South Africa's democracy, the country was often referred to as a "rainbow nation," an international exemplar of reconciliation. However, after more than two decades of democracy the term has lost its appeal. South Africans feel less like members of a "rainbow nation" and more like communities in transition, trying to find their feet in a period of stagnation and dissatisfaction at the lack of economic transformation.

Their freedom-struggle credentials won many ANC cadres positions of power in the early democratic administration, but their commitment to upliftment and progress has stalled, political corruption is rife, and key institutions are at risk of being hijacked by the State.

Sometimes South African foreign policy appears to be at odds with that of a democracy; however, the country has taken its place in the international community, and while it may have lost some of its shine under corrupt officials it continues to dominate the continent politically and economically.

South Africa is a powerhouse in Africa. It is one of the founding members of the African Union, and has the second largest economy on the continent. It is a founding member of the AU's New Partnership for Africa's Development. The Pan African parliament is situated in Midrand, and South African Dr. Nkosazana Zuma was the 2016 chairperson of the African Union.

South Africa is a member of the Southern African Development Community, the South Atlantic Peace and Cooperation Zone, the South African Customs Union, the Antarctic Treaty System, the World Trade Organization, the International Monetary Fund, G20, and G8+5. In 2010, it signed the Beijing Agreement with China, strengthening economic and political relations, and in 2011 it joined the Brazil–Russia–India–China (BRICS) alliance. It has been a key mediator in recent African conflicts, such as in Burundi, the Democratic Republic of Congo, the Comoros Islands, and Zimbabwe.

SOUTH AFRICAN CITIES

Several historical cities have been combined into eight metropolises, namely Buffalo City (East London), the City of Cape Town, Ehurhuleni Metropolitan Municipality (East Rand), the City of eThekwini (Durban), the City of Johannesburg, Mangaung Municipality (Bloemfontein), Nelson Mandela Metropolitan Municipality (Port Elizabeth), and the City of Tshwane (Pretoria).

The eight metropolises are densely populated, and there is significant centralization of economic power in Gauteng Province, and increasingly in the Cape. South Africa has always been an exporter of agricultural produce such as fruit and maize, and is a world-class manufacturer of specialized products, such as Sasol's coal/gas-to-liquid fuel technology, and an exporter of

motor vehicles. Manufacturing represents 13 percent of the gross economy, while agriculture accounts for 2.3 percent.

Ever since the discovery of gold, people have moved to Johannesburg in the hope of improving their prospects. Economic migration continues, and cities like Nelspruit, Pretoria, Durban, and Cape Town, as well as Johannesburg, receive not only internal migrants but immigrants from bordering countries, especially Zimbabwe and Mozambique. Due to the political crisis in Zimbabwe, South Africa has allowed Zimbabweans to remain on a special class of visa. Unofficial estimates of the number of Zimbabweans in South Africa range from 1.8 to 5 million.

An influx of this magnitude was bound to have an impact on the economy and on social cohesion, and has resulted in sporadic and sometimes violent outbreaks of xenophobia, with South Africans claiming that jobs are lost to foreigners who will work for less money, and blaming them for putting a strain on social services such as clinics, schools, and the like.

ISSUES

Historically, South Africans have always taken to the streets to protest, and the country has been called "the protest capital of the world." The most notable protests were against the pass laws at Sharpeville in 1960, against the imposition of Afrikaans in schools in Soweto in 1976, and more recently against low wages at the Marikana platinum mine in 2012.

Public protests have escalated since 1994. In 2014, the top three reasons for protest were the failings of the criminal justice system across the metropolises, unemployment and low salaries, and poor service delivery—the distribution of basic resources such as land, housing, water, electricity, and sanitation. The government's record in delivering and maintaining these resources and services is patchy, and in recent years protests demanding better delivery have become more widespread.

Unemployment

South Africa has the fourteenth-highest rate of unemployment in the world (26.7 percent in 2016), and the highest rate of youth unemployment (53.7 percent). While a significant portion of the youth has been educated to a basic level, they are not being employed in any great numbers. This is a result of, among other things, an education that isn't focused on skills provision; restrictive labor laws; and an industrial and manufacturing sector that is being increasingly subjected to state regulation, deterring manufacturers from taking on employees. Unemployment feeds gangsterism, drug and alcohol addiction, and crime.

Rural Poverty
Poverty is prevalent in vast swathes of rural South Africa. Infrastructure and services have still not reached these areas, and as a result a large sector of the community remains poor, uneducated, and unable to access the resources that would enable them to improve their lives, and food security is a worry.

Reform
After 1994 the ANC embarked on radical reform, with projects such as the Reconstruction and Development Programme to provide housing and electrification for disadvantaged communities. They started well with housing, mainly in urban areas, but it is apparent that delivery has stalled. The rural community still does not have access to basic amenities or health services. Life has not improved for all South Africans, and the perception of many people is that it is still the whites who are profiting from progress. Disappointment has found expression in the EFF, and as a result, their radical policies, such as political squatting (known locally as "land-grabbing"), present an attractive alternative to the ANC, who are thought to be unable or unwilling to improve their situation.

The Land Issue

Land is an enormously emotive issue in South Africa, with many black people feeling they are entitled to land they regard as having been stolen by the white man during colonialism and apartheid. The ANC has been successful in negotiating land restitution in many areas where tribes or groups were indeed removed from their land without compensation. The EFF, however, does not promote peaceful land restitution; it advocates Zimbabwe-style land-grabs where farmers in particular are kicked off their land. A form of protest adopted by the EFF has been to occupy vacant land in key visible metropolitan areas to draw attention to their cause and the issues they have gripes with. These policies are not in line with the Constitution, and a legislative framework is already in place to address legitimate land claims.

Crime

South Africa has one of the highest levels of violent crime in the world, and often its overstretched police force lacks the necessary resources or skills to tackle it. Crime is exacerbated by high levels of drug and alcohol abuse, leading to gang warfare, assaults, and murder. Economic hardship is also a driver. However, crime is becoming more sophisticated and organized today and is increasingly targeting the rich. Additionally, the justice system's strong human rights and constitutional protection provisions result in repeat offending: the law works on an "innocent until proven guilty" premise, and proof is often lacking to bring the criminals to book. The police are unable, and in some cases unwilling, to investigate cases, and different areas of the country have widely different methods of law enforcement.

HIV/AIDS

UNAIDS reported in 2015 that 7 million South Africans (19.2 percent) were HIV positive, despite educational campaigns and medical advances in treatment. Commentators blame this on sexualization at a young age, due in part to close living conditions for the vast majority of the population; homosexuality, which is still taboo, even though gay rights are recognized in the Constitution; men and women who refuse to use condoms or practice safe sex; and more recently the rise of the "blesser," or sugar daddy, a well-off older man who provides gifts and favors to poorer young women. Blessers are by no means sexually faithful, and their sexual health status is unknown. Health care workers believe this phenomenon has led to a recent spike in the spread of the disease among women, who have the highest rate of infection.

Corruption

Corruption is ongoing and insidious, from the lowest to the highest levels of government. The Public Prosecutor has faced enormous obstruction, to the point of the office facing erosion of its powers. There have been many successful investigations against the government and the office continues to function. The existence of strong opposition parties, a vocal populace, and a strong Public Prosecutor means that South Africans can be hopeful that corrupt politicians will not undermine the democratic and state institutions, in spite of their efforts to prevent their corruption from becoming public knowledge.

chapter two

VALUES & ATTITUDES

THE NEW SOUTH AFRICA

During the years of apartheid there were deep political, social, and cultural divisions, but after the release of Nelson Mandela it seemed that South Africans had had enough of separation and were committed to building a united society.

The apartheid government had done an excellent job of separating people along every line possible, except maybe for religion, and the enforcement of "separate development" precluded the creation of a common national identity. Under Mandela the new ANC government took several important steps to heal and unite this fragmented society.

A new flag was designed, giving South Africans something that they could all identify with. Flags are an emotive national symbol in South Africa, especially in the conservative Afrikaans community, with many

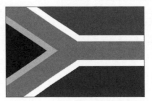

still displaying the flags of the old Boer republics in their homes, always mindful of their heritage. The pre-1994 flag certainly held no appeal for black South Africans, comprised as it was of the orange, white, and blue horizontal bands of the Dutch House of Orange, with the British Union Flag flanked by the Boer republic flags in the central white band. The presentation of a new flag reflecting the history of all of the country's people found ready acceptance among most South Africans, except in some die-hard, right-wing Afrikaans families.

A new national anthem was adopted in 1997 to be more representative of the population. Stanzas from the existing anthem, "The Call of South Africa," were retained, and parts of "Nkosi Sikelele Afrika" (God Bless Africa), a hymn written in the 1890s by Enoch Sontonga, were included. The lyrics are sung in Xhosa, Zulu, Sesotho, Afrikaans, and English, the five most widely spoken of South Africa's official languages.

Heritage Day, the national public holiday held annually on September 24, was previously known as Shaka Day in honor of the Zulu king. It was later adapted to celebrate the diversity and unity of the population. It is widely celebrated with a *braai* (barbecue), with many calling it National Braai Day, and endorsement by the National Heritage Council in 2007 as Braai4Heritage Day.

With these unifying initiatives in place, Archbishop Desmond Tutu coined the phrase "the rainbow nation," which gave the world the idea that South Africans were united in the pursuit of freedom and harmony. This was enhanced when President Mandela donned the national rugby jersey and the Springboks were victorious in the 1994 Rugby World Cup.

Probably the most important of the nation-building projects was the Constitution, which enshrines a Bill of Rights and became law in 1996. Although the constitution was drawn up in the Constitutional Assembly, formed by the National Assembly and the Senate, it was based on the ideas of ordinary citizens and political parties, and is considered to be the embodiment of the collective wisdom of South Africans. The founding provisions emphasize the unity of the country; human dignity; the equality of all people; the advancement of human rights and freedoms; nonracism and nonsexism; the supremacy of the constitution and the rule of law; universal adult suffrage; a national common voters roll; regular elections; and a multiparty system of democratic government.

Undeniably, the "rainbow nation" metaphor, the new national flag and anthem, Heritage Day, and the constitution have played significant roles in the transition to post-apartheid South Africa. For the best part of the first twenty years of full democracy, most South Africans have lived in harmony and have developed a sense of national pride and identity, but it would be unrealistic to believe that complete unity has been achieved.

This is a multifaceted but divided heterogeneous society, characterized by racial, ethnic, cultural, linguistic, and religious differences that coincide with widespread poverty and inequality. Since the early 2000s, people have been questioning whether it is actually possible to submerge their unique personal identities—and, in the case of the majority, their disadvantaged state—into a common national identity, and even whether "South African-ness" is feasible.

Racial tensions are increasing. Issues of social or economic disadvantage consistently turn into questions of race—for example, by white students who feel discriminated against by the quota governing admission to universities, and by black students who feel that because their parents were disadvantaged, they have the extra burden of struggling with fees. These areas of tension alienate people further.

While the government has passed legislation to prevent injustice, there has been less success in influencing individual behavior. Moreover, different social and ethnic groups are increasingly attaching value to their own identities and cultures, and it seems that a frank acknowledgment of these differences, rather than striving for the unity of the "rainbow nation," would be a more realistic way of promoting social cohesion and harmony.

SOUTH AFRICAN SOCIETY

Citizens of a new multiracial country with roots in a highly divided past, South Africans are still struggling to form the pillars of a post-1994 national identity. Despite the introduction of unifying national symbols, there is no overarching national narrative that makes sense of their circumstances, nor a common tradition reaching into the present. "South African society" seems to be an abstraction, characterized only by generalizations. People sometimes say, "You have to be born here to understand us," meaning that outsiders cannot begin to grasp the complexities of the country's diversity and its problems. However, there are certain shared values common to all South Africans.

Ubuntu

Ubuntu is a Nguni Bantu word, broadly meaning "human kindness." African historian Michael Onyebuchi Eze defines *ubuntu* as "A person is a person through other people," while Archbishop Tutu proposes that *ubuntu* "demands that you forgive, because resentment and anger and desire for revenge undermine harmony." *Ubuntu* forms the basis of South Africa's constitution.

As the common glue of this multicultural society, *ubuntu* defines South Africans and how they relate to others. It is the philosophy that helped shape the new government's attempt to forge a national consciousness. It is recognized in the Bill of Responsibilities, launched by the Department of Basic Education and the National Religious Leaders Forum, and in the Batho Pele (People First) principles as part of the vision and mission of transformation of the public service sector. It formed the basis on which the 1996–98 Truth and Reconciliation hearings were conducted. It is reflected in the coat of arms, and is the philosophy behind the Charter of Positive Values and the Moral Regeneration Movement adopted in 2008. Companies and institutions base their corporate philosophy on *ubuntu*, and it has become applicable in many spheres of life.

THE TRUTH AND RECONCILIATION COMMISSION

The Truth and Reconciliation Commission was a unique, court-like body that aimed at giving restorative justice to the victims of gross human rights violations during apartheid. The victims were invited to give testimony about their experiences. Likewise, the perpetrators could provide statements and request amnesty from civil and criminal prosecution. The hearings were profoundly moving and often cathartic. They were regarded as a crucial part of the transition to full democracy and, while not perfect, they are considered to have been a success.

Socially, *ubuntu* provides the framework of South African values, drawing on the ethos of an equal South Africa. It encourages a spirit of giving and contributing; of duty, accountability, and responsibility; of respect and decency; of tolerance and understanding; of integrity, loyalty, kindness, and compassion.

Visitors can be assured of South Africans' kindness in dealing with strangers. South African hospitality is an extension of this generosity; it is a willingness to assist without the expectation of profit or reward. It is almost a way of being a South African.

Sadly, there have been occasions when South Africans have not demonstrated this kindness or fellowship to foreigners. In recent years, xenophobia directed against African and Asian foreigners has broken out in the big cities, resulting in death and mayhem. These incidents usually occur in poor, overcrowded areas, where unemployment is high, there are massive frustrations and resentments, and people who have had no help from the government turn on those who are surviving and making a living in spite of difficult circumstances—the migrants.

FAMILY TIES

The nuclear family, the extended family, and the tribe are the basic units of South African society. While the nuclear family provides emotional and financial support for whites and Coloureds, the extended family provides the same support in traditional African society and in some Indian communities. However, in traditional African culture the tribe is considered the most important community.

Today, as is happening across the world, the family is being disrupted by social and economic pressures. Families become fragmented as they move away from traditional homes and villages, although at Easter and Christmas they make an effort to be together. With improved public transportation and access to independent transportation, and with cell phone technology, it is easier for people to keep in touch, but families are less able to influence members' behavior in upholding traditional values and beliefs. As a strong, functioning, and balanced family positively affects an individual's happiness, so people in dysfunctional families tend to be less satisfied with life and more inclined toward antisocial behavior.

CHILD-HEADED HOUSEHOLDS AND ORPHANS

South Africa's HIV/AIDS epidemic means that many children have been orphaned. Often these orphans live in the townships, without access to an extended family, and the children take charge of the household. Also, in some rural areas, parents are forced to move to the city to find work, and their children are left to fend for themselves, in the hope that the extended family will keep an eye on them.

However, it is children in the urban areas who find it most onerous to be the head of a household. Very often the eldest child, aged anywhere between nine and seventeen, is forced to abandon school in order to take care of his or her siblings, or of ailing parents, and the household. While the number of child-headed households hovers just under 1 percent, this represents about 50,000–90,000 families.

PATRIOTISM

Probably second only to the importance of family is the importance of the country and its affairs. South Africans are deeply political and fiercely loyal to their country and, while they are aware of its faults and shortcomings, they will always stand up for it.

The 2016 municipal elections showed that while young black South Africans are optimistic about the future, they tend not to vote. Only 500,000 eighteen- and nineteen-year-olds registered to vote—1.92 percent of 26.3 million registered voters. According to a recent survey, they feel that protests are more effective. Seeing that despite their parents' and grandparents' loyalty to the ANC little progress has been made in the delivery and quality of services, they have concluded that engaging in the democratic process is not the best way to change their lives.

In an attempt to boost patriotism in schools, the government has promoted the singing of the national anthem twice a day and has installed flags in all educational institutions.

PARTY ALLEGIANCE

Understandably, the ANC enjoys significant popularity as the party most prominent in the struggle to end apartheid. Therefore, even though it is currently failing to provide strong leadership and good governance, people continue to support it. The municipal elections of 2016 showed the first signs of disaffection with the party leadership.

Among young black people, there is a vociferous group that is committed to the idea of a more thoroughly decolonized South Africa.

"DECOLONIZATION"

"Decolonization" is a dominant political theme
today. It refers to South Africa ridding itself of the
legacy of imperialism that continues to mark the
minds of the previously colonized. The ultimate
aim of decolonization is the liberation of African
minds. To achieve this end, "fallism"—fees must
fall, Rhodes must fall—has found favor among
Africanist groups, who want to see all symbols
and repositories of colonial influence overthrown,
from the statues of mining magnate and Cape
prime minister Cecil Rhodes to the Eurocentric
syllabuses of institutions promoting the canon of
Western culture.

WORK ETHIC AND A SPIRIT OF ENTERPRISE
South Africans have a strong work ethic. Even against
the backdrop of severe unemployment, where the
formal unemployment rate hovers around 27 percent,
the spirit of enterprise flourishes.

In the industrial cities it is common to see
unemployed men and women sitting or standing in
long lines outside factories and companies in the hope
of getting a "piece job"—essentially, work for a day or
a week. Although legislation has ensured that more
black South Africans are employed, there are still very
many South Africans and foreigners without formal
employment. It is believed that the unemployment
figure is significantly higher than stated because it
doesn't take into account people who have simply
given up looking for work. Notwithstanding this
dire situation, the spirit of enterprise is strong. In
the townships and the densely populated inner cities

enterprising vendors set up shop on the sidewalks and in their homes and sell local produce, cheap Chinese goods, knockoffs, photocopied textbooks, and whatever else might turn a profit.

The average employed South African worker works 43.3 hours a week, which is the fifth-highest work rate in the world. Many work more hours than the maximum limit set by law in an attempt to augment their wages, since they may be the only breadwinner and responsible for feeding, housing, and educating their extended family. The long work day is typically complicated by the distance and long commute between the townships and the economic hubs, with many people rising at 4:00 a.m. and returning home well after 8:00 p.m.

ATTITUDES TOWARD TIME

South Africans have always been punctual, as far as circumstances allow. After 1994, with the influx of African immigrants, "Africa Time" seemed to take root in South Africa, but in the last decade or so there has been a swing back toward punctuality. And if tardiness is evident, it is usually among East and West African nationals, who seem to feel no shame at keeping clients or colleagues waiting for hours with no explanation. Having said that, it should be remembered that transportation in South Africa is often affected by traffic jams and, since most commuters use minibus taxis, if they are late for an appointment it's usually due to bad traffic or other transportation issues.

South Africans get up early in the morning to be on time for their daily activities; even in villages, the village heads reject tardiness. Politicians, however, often show total disregard for time, but use their "blue light brigade" to push their way through traffic.

EDUCATION, EDUCATION, EDUCATION

South Africans of all backgrounds place a huge emphasis on education, believing it to be the ticket to economic freedom. Parents, no matter what their economic circumstances, save up and do whatever it takes to send their children to school and on to further education. The early learning centers around the country do an excellent job of not only preparing young children for school, but also keeping them safe while their parents are at work. (See pages 109–11.)

RESPECT FOR ELDERS

Respect for elders is engrained in all South Africans. It is important to show them deference—to stand when an older person enters a room, to offer a seat if seating is limited, and to be attentive when elders speak. Some banks have designated lines or tellers that allow senior citizens to be attended to straight away, or as soon as a teller becomes available. Retirees have special benefits, such as discounts and designated days when some grocery stores and restaurants offer them special deals and quick checkout lines. Afrikaners are particularly deferential toward their elders and use the respectful terms *Oom* (uncle) and *Tannie* (aunt) to address them. When meeting African tribal leaders, visitors are advised to keep their heads lower than that of the tribal leader as a sign of respect.

TRIBALISM

For centuries colonial and post-colonial governments used a policy of "divide and rule" to manipulate and control subject peoples. The main intent of apartheid was to separate blacks and whites. The National Party used the history of tribal conflict to justify the creation of nominally autonomous "Bantustans," where tribes could develop in peace, separate from each other and from the European population. Currently in South Africa tribalism is widely called the "homeboy" phenomenon.

Tribalism, however, persists in South Africa and its tentacles have reached into politics. It became visible after 1999, during Thabo Mbeki's presidency, when "Xhosafication" meant that senior political appointments within the ANC appeared to be made according to Mbeki's Xhosa tribal affiliation, and then more recently in Jacob Zuma's "Zuluficaton" of the government, to the extent that if you aren't a Zulu member of the ANC you are unlikely to rise up the political ladder.

The politics of service delivery has become affected in certain provinces, where communities feel they are disadvantaged or ignored because of their tribe, or because their tribe isn't the tribe of the community leaders, and as a result they cannot get jobs, access services, or get their children into local schools because the language of instruction differs from their own. There are concerns that, unchecked, tribalism will produce a modern "Bantustan mentality" in the democratic South Africa.

THE URBAN–RURAL DIVIDE

In South Africa the urban population outnumbers the rural. In 2015 the urban percentage was 64.5 percent, and it is projected to reach almost 80 percent by 2050. Cities and large towns produce more than 80 percent of GDP and the metropolitan areas are growing twice as fast as the other cities. The agricultural sector accounts for only 2.3 percent of GDP, while manufacturing represents 13 percent. Two-thirds of South African youth live in urban areas because they offer higher than average incomes, and 75 percent of all jobs are created in the metros.

To manage the flow from the rural areas to the cities, the two are becoming linked by improved communications and transportation systems. The scale of migration to the cities, by both internal and external migrants, however, means that the urban spaces are unable to cope. Informal settlements spring up in the inner city, where abandoned buildings have been hijacked by migrant groups, and on the city outskirts, where thousands of shacks are built on top of one another, leaving no room for essential services to get to them should an emergency arise. The failure to design and manage South Africa's urban spaces has left people vulnerable to violence and crime.

There is a clash between the values of rural and urban dwellers. Young people living in the urban areas are more likely to stay in school than their rural counterparts; overall, girls in the rural areas are the least likely to complete their schooling.

Rural communities, both black and white, are still rooted in their respective traditions, and their world views tend to be restricted compared to those of city dwellers, who tend to integrate their new experiences and influences with their roots, and are more open to new ideas. Rural communities value human decency and reject the materialism that has become such a feature of urban society, especially in the townships.

Many young blacks want to be seen as urbane and hip, and have embraced the consumerism of city life. In cities the pace is fast, and people are ambitious and often ruthless, and this affects their behavior, since they feel compelled to keep up appearances at all costs.

PATRIARCHY

While the South African constitution may recognize the rights of all, patriarchy is still a dominant feature of the social and psychological landscape. Both black and white societies have strong patriarchal traditions. Assumptions of male supremacy and entitlement continue to oppress and exploit women. Men hold the power, in spite of much progressive legislation. Patriarchy is especially prevalent in rural areas where people have less access to education, and where the male-dominated culture rules out the possibility of women being considered equals. The president is a patriarchal practicing polygamist.

The male sense of entitlement has resulted in severe social problems and the exclusion of women from the economic mainstream, although this is changing for educated women who are becoming more visible in previously male-dominated occupations. Patriarchal values contribute to the high level of violence against women and place them at increased risk of HIV/AIDS.

GENDER ROLES

Traditionally in South Africa men held power in the community and were the providers, and women were submissive nurturers and homemakers. During apartheid white men held all the power and black males felt emasculated and were often unable to fulfill their roles as providers.

In developed countries today traditional gender roles are breaking down, but this is not the case in South Africa. After 1994, some black men began to look for ways to regain their power and self-esteem. Their assertiveness clashed with the aspirations of black women enjoying new protection in the constitution and who, feeling capable of stepping out of their prescribed roles, were challenging male power. Men lacking a strong sense of personal identity, or who are poorly educated and feel threatened by independent women, tend to push back, often violently. In South Africa they are often supported by communities that subscribe to traditional gender roles.

THE ROLE OF WOMEN

On August 9 every year, during Women's Month, South Africa commemorates Women's Day as a tribute to the 20,000 women who marched to the Union Buildings in Pretoria on that date in 1956 to protest against the extension of the notorious Pass Laws to women. This historic event showed that women had become equal partners in the struggle against apartheid.

It was women who petitioned the white prime ministers to end apartheid. They pioneered women's movements, such as the ANC Women's League in 1913 and the Black Sash in 1955, and encouraged women to engage in the struggle for freedom. In 1946 seven women were among the seventeen resisters who occupied the site in Umbilo Road in Durban in the Passive Resistance Campaign against the Ghetto Act of 1946, which restricted Indian ownership of property. Many other, predominantly black, women played important roles in standing united against apartheid. These women and their children, such as Winnie Mandela and Gertrude Shope, were usually separated from their husbands, who either worked away from home, or were in exile or eluding the police.

Over and above the political hardships they endured, they had to contend with the additional drawback of being women in a patriarchal society, where women were not encouraged to study or work outside the home. In rural areas women didn't consider doing anything without their husbands' permission. This wasn't limited to black women, but extended to Afrikaans families, where the man was, and to a large extent still is, regarded as the head of the family.

Since 1994, there have been changes for women in all spheres of society. Many have become leaders in sectors previously dominated by men, such as medicine and engineering. Their most notable achievement is that they were involved in drawing up the constitution and deciding how the country should be governed.

Before 1994 women had a paltry 2.7 percent representation in the white parliament; they currently occupy 41 percent of parliamentary seats. Many acts have been passed to improve the lives of women, even if their provisions are not always carried out. In 2014, a dedicated Ministry for Women in the Presidency was established to elevate women's issues and interests, and to oversee transformation in women's socio-economic empowerment, rights, and equality.

Women have also held important international roles, such as Dr. Nkosazana Dlamini-Zuma, as the first woman to chair the African Union Commission in 2012, and Judge Navi Pillay, as a judge in the International

Criminal Court. Public Protector Thuli Madonsela gained the confidence and trust of South Africans in standing firm against corruption and state capture of South African institutions in 2016. Female judges make up almost 30 percent of the judiciary, and 40 percent of senior management in the public service sector. However, in the corporate sector they constitute only about 3.6 percent of CEOs, 5.5 percent of chairperson positions, and 17.1 percent of directorships.

Although significant progress has been made in the political, public, and corporate spheres, poor women remain marginalized. Even so, while most South African women continue to be the nurturers and supporters of men, they are now more ambitious and strive to improve their own and their families' lives by being productive members of society.

It is unfortunate that crimes against women in South Africa still go largely unpunished, with the perpetrators often being given the benefit of the doubt. Laudable initiatives to raise awareness have had little impact on the serious issue of violence against women. In 2007–13 there were more than a million "contact" crimes (violence or threats of violence) against women in which the women knew the perpetrators, and it is assumed that this is a mere fraction of the real number since women are notoriously unlikely to report crimes of violence against themselves. In 2015–16, 42,596 rapes were reported; it is believed that the figures don't reflect the actual number. Domestic abuse is still an issue and is no easier to resolve in post-apartheid South Africa, since many women will not go against their culture by shaming their husbands.

Recently the Department of Home Affairs automatically changed newly married women's surnames to their husbands' names. Since women have the legal right to retain their maiden names they have rejected this, and have taken the matter to the Equality Court. The matter is still ongoing.

CHILDREN

Children have an added importance in South Africa. Because of the painful past, a lot is invested in them. Many rural families still consider children to be their future wealth—their retirement policies—while urban South Africans are well aware of the cost of raising a child. The proverb might say that it takes a village to raise a child, but most people know that it takes money, and the size of families has decreased. South Africans seem to strike a good balance between love and discipline. However, unless they live in isolated areas, most South African children grow up being fairly aware of crime and are street-wise. They are also usually friendly and curious. Most black children make their own way to and from school, dodging traffic and people with criminal intentions. Most white children are chauffeured everywhere, and don't have the street-smarts of their black compatriots. (See page 107.)

The constitution protects the rights of children, and states that they should have equal access to education, housing, and care, but these rights are provided only insofar as their families or legal guardians are able to do so. Before 1994 there were many public and private institutions that offered refuge for vulnerable children—street children who had escaped from abusive or neglectful parents, or who had become hooked on drugs or lured into prostitution. Unfortunately, due to incidents of abuse in supposed places of safety, the Children's Act was amended, and children can no longer be simply taken off the streets and put into care. Instead, the law requires a social worker to interview the child, write a report, and submit it to the court, which makes a decision on whether or not the child can be placed in protective custody. This has had grave consequences for the very children the Act was intended to protect. Children who did not have a court order were removed from such facilities, their education came to a halt, and they returned to the streets. As a result, there are many young children, mainly boys, who live on the streets, often turning to crime and/or drugs and prostitution to keep hunger at bay. These children are most at risk of being victims of crime and social misfortune.

Many childcare centers now provide skills training and offer street children a hot meal, but these are only open during office hours. However desperate their plight, it is ultimately more helpful to donate money to these centers than to give cash to the street children, who then find it quite lucrative to become beggars.

THE GENERATION GAP
In South Africa 66 percent of the population are between fourteen and thirty-four years of age.

Millennials (those born since 1983) are generally optimists who value diversity and are willing to cooperate, work, and learn—if they've had advantages. However, a vast number of these young people aren't operating in the economy, are less inclined to cooperation and optimism, and, in fact, are angry. Education is still largely unaffordable for most black South Africans, thus denying many the opportunity to fulfill their potential.

The Baby Boomers and Generation Xers—the parents and grandparents of the millennials—have a very different world view. In South Africa the Baby Boomers redefined traditional values, and think of themselves as a hard-working generation. Generation Xers are inclined to be strong individuals, possibly due to the sharpening of the issues in 1961, with the declaration of a Republic by white South Africans and the formation of the ANC's armed wing Umkhonto We Sizwe in the same year.

As a result of the ending of apartheid in 1994, millennials are more inclined to have diverse groups of friends and to tackle challenges together; they use social media effectively; and they are more confident than their predecessors. Not having experienced the worst of apartheid, they see no reason to ask for their rights, or protest quietly, believing instead that they are fully entitled to what has been promised in the Constitution. Whereas their parents were frugal, hardworking, and believed that tenacity helped you achieve your goals, it would appear that many millennials feel entitled and angry, and will not be denied.

"Born Frees" are black South Africans who were born after the 1994 elections. They acknowledge the importance of the Struggle, but they are focused on the future, and are dismissive of their grandparents' and parents' patience in waiting for transformation. They believe the future belongs to them, whether or not political and social progress keeps pace. They don't believe in a "rainbow nation," and question why the country's wealth is still in the hands of the whites.

CONSUMERISM

South Africa is a consumer society. Since 1994 all the multinational brands have returned and have found a willing market—people who felt deprived during the years of boycotts and who are now only too happy to spend their money on designer labels, celebrity concerts, and fancy cars. Wealth is particularly aspired to in the townships, especially among the youth, who feel that it differentiates them from their country cousins.

Some parents, especially those who grew up poor, will get into debt for their children, not only to provide an education but often so that they won't feel different from their more affluent peers. Some feel that by buying their children stuff they are helping them to fit in better, and keeping them from stealing, and so out of jail. These indulged children don't take no for an answer, and feed their parents' fears that they will become gang members or drug dealers if their demands are not met.

SEXUAL ATTITUDES

Traditional morality still prevails, to some degree, in rural areas, but as more and more South Africans become urbanized there has been a definite breakdown in sexual mores. Most South Africans are young, and their sexual behavior reflects current global trends. Virgnity is not the prize it was in the last century. Most young people do not marry until their late twenties or early thirties, and are sexually active without the commitment of marriage.

Many South Africans have children out of wedlock, and this is generally not frowned upon, even though it may be challenging to bring children up alone. Single black women, however, bemoan the attitude of many black men who are sexually promiscuous but don't use protection against pregnancy and STDs, and who don't stay around to look after any offspring that might result from their relationships.

Although polygamy is not a constitutional right, it is legal in the case of a man in a customary marriage who wishes to marry a second wife. He simply has to apply to the court for such a marriage to be legal, under the provisions of the Recognition of Customary Marriages Act. Women may not be polyandrous.

Prostitution has been illegal in South Africa since 1957, but the law was amended in 2007 to criminalize clients who frequent prostitutes. This has not stopped the practice, which is found in town and country alike.

HIV/AIDS is a major national health issue and there is still much stigma attached to those who are HIV positive. Many people still refer to the illness obliquely, in terms such as "that sick." (See page 99.)

ATTITUDES TOWARD SEXUAL MINORITIES

Traditional social and religious norms in South Africa left little room for tolerance, let alone understanding, of sexual minorities. Before 1994 male homosexuality was against the law, though lesbianism was not (possibly because in a patriarchy it was inconceivable). The 1996 constitution was the first in the world to outlaw discrimination based on sexual orientation, and South Africa was the fifth country in the world to legalize same-sex marriage. Same-sex couples are allowed to adopt children jointly and may legally engage in IVF and surrogacy programs.

Despite this progressive legislation, attitudes take longer to change, and LGBT South Africans still face social hostility, and in extreme cases acts of violence. Black Christian communities are vehemently opposed to LGBT practices and are vocal in their condemnation of them. Lesbians have it particularly hard in the black townships, where groups of men have been known to rape lesbians to "sort them out" (so-called "corrective rape"). In 2000, the Promotion of Equality and Prevention of Unfair Discrimination Act established special Equality Courts to address discrimination experienced by private individuals.

Prominent public figures such as Archbishop Tutu (whose own daughter is a lesbian) have voiced their support for the LGBT community, and even the Calvinist Dutch Reformed Church has ruled that LGBT people can hold positions of authority in the Church and should not be discriminated against.

Despite the occasional incidents of homophobia, gay people living in the major urban areas are generally accepted. Cape Town boasts of being the gay capital of Africa and celebrates Gay Pride, as does Johannesburg. Knysna, in the western Cape, hosts the Pink Loerie Mardi Gras, attracting gay people from across the country. Gay relationships feature in television programs, such as the local soap "Egoli." South Africa welcomes gay tourists, and there are gay-friendly establishments throughout the country—the Pink Route stretches from Cape Town to Johannesburg and on to the Kruger National Park. There is no doubt that local businesses value gay patrons, whose money is locally termed the "Pink Rand.

SOCIAL MOBILITY
The Burgeoning Black Middle Class

The growth of South Africa's new middle class since 1994 means that it now comprises 17 percent of the population. Blacks make up 51 percent, whites 34 percent, Coloureds 9 percent, and Indians 6 percent. These statistics are a far cry from the old days of white supremacy. In 2017 the average black person's income went up by 14.9 percent per year while the average white person's income rose by 5.3 percent. Many of the black high earners work in the civil service, in which blacks represent 75 percent of all employees.

The ANC government has worked hard to reduce the disparity between whites and blacks, and has become a major employer. A job in the public sector is a status symbol in the black community, since, among other benefits, it is seen as a job for life.

In spite of all the advances made, however, it is very difficult for poor black people to join the middle class because of the obstacles they face in education, access to health care, job opportunities, and the like.

The purchasing power of the black middle class has undoubtedly benefited the economy. The members of this affluent community came to be called "Black Diamonds", but due to the newly wealthy tycoons and celebrities' bad behavior making the daily news, it has since become a derogatory term for those who consume without restraint, show poor taste in dress and behavior, are oblivious to social problems, and ignore customary African concepts such as *ubuntu*.

The emergence of a black middle class means that traditionally white suburbs are now also home to black families, and schools in the suburbs are fully integrated. The black townships have seen little to no integration.

Poor Whites

After the Anglo-Boer War, many Afrikaners were left destitute, without homes or families. These dispossessed people became known as "poor whites," and by 1929 (pre-Depression) 300,000 of the one million Afrikaners were assumed to be living at pauper level. However, industrial growth was a godsend to the uprooted communities who flocked to the cities in search of work. When the National Party came to power in 1948, they made a concerted effort to employ unskilled Afrikaners in government institutions, and this boosted their economic status, effectively reducing the number of poor whites. Post-1994, there is once again a group of poor whites, who are estimated to number in the region of 82,000 (2016), which is negligible compared to 25 million poor blacks. Some white right-wingers hold up these poor whites as an example of "genocide" against the whites, when in fact their relatively low number is an unexceptionable demographic percentage.

The Dominant Class

There are a number of different groups that compete for the country's wealth. There are the well-established, white super-rich, who have used the country's natural wealth to launch themselves and their conglomerates into international markets. This is the capitalist group that the EFF object to and accuse of holding all the economic power. There is the newly emergent black elite, who are politically well connected and who play a role in the control of the country's state-owned enterprises inherited from the apartheid regime. And there is another emergent black elite who, through their political connections, are the owners and controllers of large sectors of the economy, such as the core industries allied to large-scale mineral extraction, energy provision, and the associated downstream sectors, such as ESKOM (the Electricity Supply Commission).

It is these last two groups that make up South Africa's ruling class, and they determine what activities constitute transformation and what changes actually take place in South Africa. The white capitalist groups are not part of the ruling class; their interests don't feature in the transformation agenda of the ruling class.

The political elite and the economic tycoons have clashed on several occasions—the most recent being the Marikana Massacre, where neither group was willing to take responsibility for the wage strike that ended in bloodshed.

ATTITUDES TOWARD FOREIGNERS

While South Africans generally get on well with foreign nationals, there is a definite mistrust on the part of some black South Africans of African foreigners, and there have been isolated incidents of intolerance toward Asian migrants, mainly those from Pakistan, Bangladesh, and the Republic of China. This mistrust or dislike of African foreigners—caused mainly by economic jealousy and the perception that they have taken away jobs and opportunities that should be available to South Africans—has resulted in outbreaks of xenophobia that have strained relations between South Africa and the countries of origin of these migrants.

Many Americans, British people, Europeans, and Australians live and work in South Africa, and are well received. This might be because they are not considered to pose an economic threat in the way that the African and Asian foreigners are perceived to, or simply because of familiarity, given South Africa's long historical ties with Britain and Europeans.

chapter **three**

CUSTOMS
& TRADITIONS

South Africa's cultural diversity reflects the historical movement of peoples into the country. Every ethnic group brought its own concepts, beliefs, and practices. The Bantu majority consists of many different groups, each with its own identity and traditions. The Europeans are culturally rooted in their countries of origin, and the Malay slaves and indentured Indian laborers brought with them Islamic and Hindu customs and traditions.

Strong African cultural traditions survive in rural areas, but growing urbanization has resulted in the dilution of many traditional beliefs and customs among black South Africans.

RELIGIOUS DIVERSITY

South Africa is a secular state, and its Constitution guarantees freedom of religion. The dominant religion is Christianity, but African traditional religion, Judaism, Islam, Hinduism, Buddhism, and Baha'ism are present.

The traditional beliefs of the Khoi, San, and Bantu peoples underpin the forms of black traditional religion practiced today, but these have also been combined with Christianity, introduced by the Dutch and British settlers. African traditional religion has about six million followers. It practices ancestor worship, espouses *ubuntu*, focuses on special events in people's lives, such as births, initiations, weddings, and funerals, and sacrifices animals at special events and to honor the ancestors' spirits.

During colonial times there was a sweeping move by European missionaries to convert Africans to Christianity, and this continued during apartheid. Today about 80 percent of the population are Christian and belong to mainstream denominations such as Catholicism, Anglicanism, Methodism, and Presbyterianism, as well as the Afrikaans Protestant Churches and the independent African Christian Churches. Even the smallest, most remote town is likely to have an impressive church, usually Dutch Reformed.

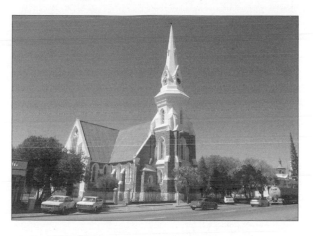

Approximately four million South Africans are Roman Catholic. Most white Catholics are descended from Irish immigrants; there are also descendants of Second World War Italian prisoners of war, and many Portuguese, who came from Angola and Mozambique after independence there in the 1970s. There are many black Catholics, but very few Asian Catholics.

Most white South African Christians are Protestants, and the largest Protestant denomination is the Pentecostal movement, followed by Methodists, the Dutch Reformed Church, and Anglicans.

The most popular black Christian Church is the Zion Christian Church (ZCC), which has its headquarters at Zion City in Moria, in Limpopo Province—there are usually long lines of buses outside its facility, backing up traffic for miles during the Easter weekend festivities. The ZCC was established in 1910, and has a membership of close to ten million.

Greek and Russian Orthodox Churches have been established for decades and continue to be important in the lives of Greek and Russian immigrants, both for worship and for celebrating major family milestones.

Foreign African nationals, such as Nigerians, have established charismatic Churches in the major metropolitan areas. They have regular weekly services that are loud and energetic, usually include some form of faith-healing, and encourage tithing.

Although Islam is a minority religion, beautiful mosques are found across the country and a large

number of South African Indians are Muslim. Since 1994, Muslim economic migrants have arrived from Somalia, Pakistan, India, and more recently Bangladesh. The number of converts to Islam is increasing as more people are drawn to it, especially in deprived areas where Islamic welfare agencies assist the poor by providing food and education. The majority of South African Muslims are Sunni.

A number of Jews migrated to the Cape in the 1820s, but the Jewish community grew dramatically between 1880 and 1914, coming mainly from the Pale of Settlement in Tsarist Russia—in particular from Lithuania. During apartheid and subsequent to 1994, many South African Jews emigrated to the UK, North America, Australia, and Israel, and in many South African towns where Jews were once the lifeblood of the economy there are abandoned synagogues. There are still sizable Jewish communities in the large cities.

South Africa has the second-largest concentration of Hindus in Africa. Its most notable Hindu resident was Mahatma Ghandi, who petitioned the government for permission to build the first Hindu crematorium in Johannesburg, to enable Hindus to cremate their dead according to custom. The first Hindu temples were built in the 1870s, but in 1910 temple building and property ownership by Hindus were prohibited. Today there are many temples where Hindu communities observe their festivals. Driving through the remaining sugar cane fields in KZN, the billowing colorful flags that adorn even the most modest of temples are a common sight.

There is an impressive Buddhist temple in Bronkhorstspruit, Gauteng, built by the Taiwanese Fo Guang Shan Buddhist order in the late 1990s. This has become a national tourist destination, but is very much a working temple.

TRADITIONAL AFRICAN BELIEFS

In traditional African religion the natural world is suffused with spiritual power, often seen as a host of spirits controlled by a Supreme Being. There are no scriptures. The religion is transmitted orally, handed down through the generations in the form of myths and stories that shape the worldview of African people. It is concerned with cosmology, ritual, and society, and is expressed in customs, ceremony, and everyday life.

Of great importance is the link between the living and the world of the ancestors: the belief that we can maintain a constant relationship with that world. Thus ancestor worship is an extension of the respect for elders. Followers believe that they are guided by their ancestors' spirits, and involve them in every major event, such as births, weddings, and deaths—it's common for university graduation ceremonies to be punctuated by ululating and thanks being offered to the ancestors.

The most important aspect of African religion is the community, made up of people who share the same traditions. The belief system aims to enhance human values, support moral order, and create a sense of security—the individual is totally defined by the community, and nonconformity is perceived as a threat. In most communities there are spiritual leaders who are responsible for its spiritual and religious survival. Women are key players in the upholding of tradition.

Traditional believers ask their ancestors to intercede with the Supreme Being on their behalf. The ancestral spirits become unhappy or angry when their descendants stray, and so they usually make offerings of meat or beer to appease them. It is common practice to slaughter an animal as an offering or to celebrate important occasions.

Sangomas, or traditional healers, are responsible for divining, counseling, foretelling the future, and summoning ancestors. They undergo a thorough training in the use of medicinal herbs, and employ occult skills to help solve social problems, or even sometimes to locate missing objects.

The most feared evil spirit among black communities is the *tokoloshe*, a potentially malevolent imp that usually gets up to mischief at night. In many black homes it was usual to elevate beds on empty paint cans or bricks, so that the feared *tokoloshe* wouldn't be able to get on to the bed and terrorise the sleeping occupant. A local newspaper, *The Daily Sun*, regularly carries stories of the *tokoloshe*, adding fuel to the fires of fear. Most educated and enlightened blacks no longer hold these fears.

South Africans pride themselves on their religious tolerance, and even though the missionaries and the apartheid regime sought converts to Christianity, people were nevertheless free to worship in their own way, largely without interference.

BIRTHS

In all communities the birth of a child is hailed as a continuation of life. Traditionally, childbirth confers status and social recognition on the mother. Expectant mothers in rural areas are encouraged to approach natural childbirth without fear, and are aided in this by having a family member or their extended family present at the birth. An animal is traditionally slaughtered as a thanksgiving sacrifice and its skin is given to the new infant. Naming ceremonies are important in some tribes, and this connects the baby to the ancestors who have gifted the child with talents.

Urban South African women usually give birth in hospitals and, given the poor quality of state health care, most women who can afford it choose to deliver in "boutique" maternity hospitals. State hospitals are nevertheless a necessity for most, and are also the destination for women from neighboring countries where maternal health care is inadequate or nonexistent. The under-five mortality rate is 45.1 deaths per 1,000 live births (2015).

Judaism, Christianity, and Islam—the three Abrahamic religions—share similar birth rituals.

COMING-OF-AGE CEREMONIES

Coming-of-age ceremonies are the gateway to full membership of the community. In African culture the initiation of young men into adulthood is usually accompanied by the practice of circumcision, which may take place some time after the onset of puberty up to the age of about twenty, but is usually done between the ages of twelve and sixteen. While there are commonalities in the ceremonies, there are also subtle differences between the different tribes. Young Xhosa men are painted in white clay and wrapped in blankets when they return from having spent several days "in the bush" (which is how the ceremony is referred to). Sotho men are sent to stay in a secluded lodge with several other initiates. They are circumcised and instructed on how to conduct themselves as adults. In many tribes, if a man has not been initiated, he is not considered to be a real man. This attitude results in pressure being brought to bear on young men who aren't convinced of the need for circumcision. A

major downside to the practice is the lack of expertise of the traditional circumcisers, who may use rusty knives or dull blades, and who can not only mutilate young men but cause death from infection due to unsterilized equipment. Health officials offer their services and/or sterilized equipment to circumcisers to ensure safe and hygienic operations, but many traditionalists prefer to work in the old way, without interference.

In some communities women also have a ceremonial initiation into adulthood. This is a spiritual and practical induction into the expectations that society has of women, not a physical marking of their passage into adulthood. One such initiation is the Zulu Reed Dance, based on the older Swazi Umcwasho traditional chastity rite, where young women wearing traditional dress collect and present the Zulu king with cut reeds. It takes place over several days in September at the eNyokeni Palace in Nongoma, Zululand, and involves singing, dancing, and other activities designed to prepare Zulu girls for womanhood.

MARRIAGE

Three types of marriage are recognized in South African law. Civil marriages are carried out by licenced marriage officers at magistrates' courts, or by religious marriage officers in churches or wedding chapels. Civil marriages took a dip during the 2008 financial crisis and continue to decline, with fewer than 160,000 recorded in 2013. Customary marriages (following tribal law) include polygamous unions and have also declined, to 3,498 in 2013. Civil unions include same-sex marriage and are the only type of union to have risen in number, from 760 in 2009 to 993 in 2013. From these statistics it would appear that South Africans are content to be common-law partners rather than formalize their unions.

Statistics aside, weddings are a time when South Africans join their families and friends to celebrate. But before a wedding can even be planned in a traditional black family, the *lobola* (bride price) has to be negotiated by the bride's and groom's elders. It is customary for the groom to pay the bride's family a dowry. Traditionally this was paid in cattle, but nowadays it is equally common to pay in cash or kind.

There's no template for South African weddings. Generally people favor the warmer months—September to December. Black South Africans are likely to get married during the Easter period or over the Christmas holidays, continuing the tradition from apartheid times when they could get time off work to return to their traditional lands to get married. The large urban black population still has strong ties to its ancestral homelands, and young upwardly mobile black people are

likely to return home for their wedding, or have a wedding "at home" and another celebration in the township, depending on what they can afford. Coloured families celebrate much like their white counterparts, or like Muslims, depending on their religious or cultural affiliation.

Of course, all wedding couples wear their finest, whether it is a traditional Western white wedding dress, beads and skins for Zulu brides, or an Indian red sari. Some couples choose to follow family traditions and others create their own.

Although traditional black wedding ceremonies are similar to each other, there are variations. A Xhosa woman inserts a knife into the ground, indicating her acceptance of a marriage proposal. During the day of the wedding, the groom and bride are separated; men sit on chairs and women on the floor. A Ndebele groom's mother will make a *jocolo* (goatskin apron) that is worn by married women during the ceremony. A Zulu bride will change her outfit up to three times during the day to impress her in-laws.

After the ceremony, the Zulu wedding party will go to the groom's family compound to slaughter a cow, and the bride will place money inside the cow's stomach to symbolize her joining the new family.

Jewish, Muslim, and Hindu religious practices are much the same as they are in other countries. Indian (Hindu) and Cape Malay (Muslim) weddings are particularly colorful, and can last for several days.

DEATH

In traditional African belief death, while inevitable, was not part of God's original plan. Yet, by death a person becomes an ancestor, provided he has had children, has died in an appropriate way, and has been correctly buried.

In the early days after losing a loved one, black Christian families grieve openly and are generally supported by the wider family and friends. Burial takes place from a few days to a week after death. During this period, family and friends commiserate with the bereaved and usually bring flowers and food before the funeral and on the day itself.

Depending on the wishes of the deceased, the type of death, and the culture of the family, the coffin is left open or closed for the night vigil. On the day of the funeral, it is placed either at home or in a church, where anyone who would like to pay their last respects can do so. The funeral service may be held in the church or at the graveside. After the ceremony, the body may be buried or cremated. It is customary to offer mourners food and drink after the burial, which, depending on the family's means, may be tea and snacks, a drink and something to eat at a pub, or a full meal at which an animal may be slaughtered.

FEAST DAYS AND FESTIVALS

South Africans love getting together to celebrate. There are hundreds of colorful festivals throughout the year, ensuring that everyone gets a chance to make the most of what's available—sports, music, theater, cultural experiences, floral displays, and literary events. The different ethnic groups also enjoy their own cultural celebrations, such as the Zulu Reed Dance, Burns Night, Diwali, and Greek Easter.

January 2: The Cape Town Minstrel Carnival

The perfect start to the New Year, this is a one-day event that takes place annually in Cape Town. In the early nineteenth century slaves were allowed a day off work to usher in the New Year in their own way. After emancipation, the *Tweede Nuwe Jaar* ("Second New Year") became a celebration in District Six—an inner-city area made up largely of former slaves, artisans, merchants, and Cape Malays—that united the "creole culture" in Cape Town. Today, continuing the tradition, ten thousand banjo players and dancers with white-painted faces and colorful costumes parade through the city's streets until they reach Green Point Stadium, where they enter various music and dance competitions. This life-affirming musical bonanza is as much a celebration of freedom as of the New Year.

February: Chinese New Year

This can be celebrated by anyone wishing to join in the festivities in Chinatowns around the country. There are fireworks, traditional lion dances, food, and drink. Chinese families traditionally eat dumplings and long noodles to celebrate long life. Red envelopes containing new money are given to children to bless them for the coming year. If giving a gift to a Chinese person on New Year, don't give a sharp object, which suggests a desire to cut ties with them. Another unwelcome gift would be a watch, which means that you think they're running out of time. Most New Year celebrations end with extravagant fireworks to frighten away the evil spirits and welcome in the New Year.

March: The Cape Epic

This "untamed" mountain bike challenge is an eight-day event that will test even the most practiced mountain biker. It must be completed by both members of a two-person team, with only 650 teams allowed to race. The route changes annually and covers 435 miles (700 km) of breathtaking scenery, and 49,212 feet (15,000 m) of accumulated climbing of magnificent mountain passes. It is the most televised mountain bike stage race in the world, and the only eight-day mountain bike stage race classed as *hors catégorie* by the Union Cycliste Internationale, making it a highlight on the professional racer's calendar.

March: The Cape Town Festival
Held in the Company Gardens in Cape Town, the festival celebrates "one city, many cultures." It's usually a weekend of music, family, food, and fun.

March: The SciFest Africa
South Africa's annual national science festival is held in Grahamstown in the Eastern Cape. It features around six hundred events: lectures, exhibitions, workshops, theatrical productions, field trips, laser shows, quizzes, science Olympiads, shows, and tours. Over 45,000 enthusiasts attend each year.

March/April: The Two Oceans Marathon
This world-renowned athletics event takes place in the Cape over the Easter Weekend. It has different configurations to suit runners' individual race styles—from Fun Runs for kids to the 35-mile (56-km) ultra marathon for dedicated athletes.

April: The Splashy Fen Festival
This appeals to the younger crowd who are into folk and rock music, and takes place out of doors in Underberg, in the foothills of the Drakensberg. It offers bands, trail running courses, supervised children's entertainments, and a variety of artisan and craft food, handicrafts, beer gardens, and bars.

May: The Comrades Marathon
The Comrades Marathon, the world's oldest ultramarathon, grew out of the League of Comrades of the Great War, established to help families affected by the First World War, and for soldiers to reconnect and rekindle the camaraderie shared on the battlefields. One

such soldier was South African Vic Clapham, who dreamed of and proposed a marathon to the League of Comrades. The Comrades Marathon began in 1921; thirty-four aspiring athletes lined up at its start and sixteen finished. The race is now capped at 20,000 participants from across the world and is a major highlight in the international marathon diary. It is run between Pietermaritzburg and Durban, and the direction alternates every year—one year it's a "down" run, and the next year it's an "up" run.

May: The Franschhoek Literary Festival
This takes place over the third weekend in May, and is a major event in the literary calendar. International authors are flown in to join local authors for talks and conversation, and events are booked out in advance.

June/July: The Grahamstown National Arts Festival
In an eleven-day feast of arts, crafts, and entertainment, the population of the university town of Grahamstown

doubles, as 50,000 visitors flood in to experience indigenous and imported theater, dance, opera, cabaret, fine art, craft, music, poetry, jazz, and comedy. This is one of the most diverse festivals in the world. Book well in advance, especially as accommodations are limited.

July: The Knysna Oyster Festival

Appealing to oyster lovers, sports lovers, and people looking for an excuse to celebrate, this is one of South Africa's most popular festivals. There are multisports challenges, kids' races, wine tasting, and oysters and seafood for all. Much of the revenue generated bolsters local community charities.

August: The Joy of Jazz

Taking place annually in Johannesburg, the Joy of Jazz is one of the most popular jazz festivals on South Africa's musical calendar. Top local performers are joined by international artists, who perform in a variety of jazz styles at venues across the city.

September: The Namaqualand Flower Festival

In spring the dull, semi-arid northern Cape terrain is ablaze with a dazzling display of indigenous flora, attracting visitors from all over the world.

September/October: Hermanus Whale Festival

The scenic village of Hermanus on the Cape's south coast is the best land-based whale-watching destination in the world. The massive Southern Right whales are the star performers here, at the only enviro-arts festival in South Africa. Whale enthusiasts can also enjoy great food, quality arts and crafts, sports events, music events, and a marine Eco village.

October: The Cape Town International Kite Festival
This is held annually on the lawns of the Zandvlei
Nature Reserve, and attracts more than 20,000 visitors,
including international kiters, who fly their impressive
kite creations.

November: Cherry Festival
The eastern Free State town of Ficksburg hosts the
oldest crop festival in the country. There are cherry
tours, cherry product competitions, cherry bake-offs,
and cherry *mampoer* (moonshine) brewing. Craft shows
and music performances run alongside the main events.

December: The Nedbank Golf Challenge
Where the world's top golfers compete for a prestigious
trophy and a million-dollar prize. Sun City boasts two
of the best golf courses in Africa, and the challenge is
played over the Gary Player Court Club Course.

PUBLIC HOLIDAYS
South Africa has more national holidays than most
countries. Offices close and people head for the great
outdoors or spend the day with friends and family.
Banks and businesses shut down, but restaurants
and places of entertainment remain open for business.

If the date of a public holiday falls on a Sunday, the
holiday is moved to the Monday. Thus given a three-
day weekend, people head for holiday resorts across the
country and national roads become traffic-laden. If a
holiday marks a political event, such as Youth Day
(June 16), political rallies take place.

School holidays are also opportunities for leisure.
Private schools generally have three terms a year, and
state schools have four. The March/April break is the

most significant one for black families who return to their home villages or travel to religious centers to celebrate Easter. Many families head for the beach or bushveld resorts to enjoy the last of the fall sunshine before winter sets in. The June/July/August vacation is when both private and public schools break and families flock to the warm coastal resorts.

The festive break in December/January is when schools shut down and commerce comes to a halt. It's a pleasure to spend this period in inland cities where the traffic is nonexistent after the exodus to the coast, and it's easy to get a booking at a popular restaurant. From east coast to west, the country's beautiful, well-maintained beaches are filled with vacationing families, and facilities are stretched to capacity.

Celebrating at Home
The South African home is a place of refuge, and where family and friends are welcome. South Africans pride themselves on their hospitality (see page 94); however, while some people have an open-door policy,

others prefer that guests don't just turn up out of the blue. So, it's best to wait for an invitation or ask if a visit would be in order.

While South Africans happily frequent the malls and sidewalk restaurants in the trendy suburbs, they also like to socialize at home, and the South African weather really does support at-home entertaining.

THE HOLIDAY CALENDAR
January 1: New Year's Day
March 21: Human Rights Day
Commemorated annually to remind South Africans of the sacrifices that accompanied the struggle for democracy.
Friday before Easter Sunday: Good Friday
Catholic and Protestant holiday.
Day after Easter Sunday: Easter Monday, or Family Day
Easter Monday for Christians, Family Day for those who are not.

April 27: Freedom Day
Commemorates the day in 1994 when the first
fully democratic election was held, representing the
end of apartheid.

May 1: Labour Day
Celebrates the role played by trade unions, the
Communist Party, and other labor movements in
the struggle against apartheid.

June 16: Youth Day
Commemorates the Soweto Uprising of June 1976
and recognizes the role of the youth in the liberation
from the apartheid regime.

August 9: National Women's Day
Commemorates the 1956 march of 20,000 women
to the Union Buildings in Pretoria to petition against
the Pass Laws.

September 24: Heritage Day
South Africans across the spectrum celebrate the
diversity of their beliefs and traditions.

December 16: Day of Reconciliation
Instituted to foster reconciliation and unity. This
is a significant date both for the Afrikaners, who
triumphed over the Zulus at the Battle of Blood River
in 1838, and for the ANC, as it commemorates the
first actions against the apartheid regime in 1961 by
Umkhonto we Sizwe, the ANC's armed wing.

December 25: Christmas Day
Christian holiday

December 26: Day of Goodwill
This has its roots in Boxing Day (boxing up what
you don't need to give to the less fortunate), and its
name now reflects the real intention of the day

chapter four

MAKING FRIENDS

MEETING SOUTH AFRICANS

Urban South Africans are generally sociable and welcoming to strangers. Rural folk may be more guarded but are no less friendly. Most South Africans are eager to meet new people—possibly a legacy of the apartheid days, when segregation enforced separation of blacks and whites, and international disapproval isolated the country from the rest of the world.

These days, it's not unusual for foreign visitors to meet South Africans even before they arrive in the country, either via social media or through social or business networks. For their part, South Africans are generally willing to accept new people into their social circle, but it will take a few encounters for them to get to know you well enough to consider you more than an acquaintance.

You can meet South Africans in bars, through friends, at sports clubs, or in special-interest groups, such as those for hiking, cycling, or birdwatching. Rotary Clubs and Lions International also provide opportunities to meet people. Young people tend to go out and about in a crowd, so if you're invited to join them there's no need to come with a friend. They socialize in a group and enjoy things together.

GREETINGS

Offering a smile usually gets a reciprocal response. However, there are several styles of greeting, depending on ethnicity, so it's best to smile and let the other party initiate a handshake. Most South Africans will shake hands, smile, and maintain eye contact. Some women, such as Muslim and traditional African women, may just nod politely, so when in doubt wait to see if the woman offers her hand. A man and a woman who know each other well may kiss each other on the cheek, in the increasingly popular European style.

THE AFRICAN HANDSHAKE

In South Africa the elaborate "African handshake," or "comrade handshake," is a sign of respect and friendship. Whites commonly greet their black friends with it too. This is how to do it:

1. Grip the other person's hand in the common European handshake.
2. Open your hand, twist your grip slightly upward to grip the base of the other person's thumb with all your fingers.
3. Open your hand, twist your hand slightly downward and resume the common European handshake.

This may end here, or when the hand-shakers lean forward and touch opposite shoulders. It can be complicated! Wait for the person you're meeting to initiate this form of greeting, and just go with the flow.

Formal and Informal Modes of Address

Although South Africans are usually an informal lot, there are situations that call for formal salutations. It's quite acceptable to say, "Hi," "Hello," or "How's it going?" to someone you're meeting informally or who you know quite well. Formally, you'd extend a hand and say "Hello, I'm pleased to meet you," and introduce yourself.

If you're meeting elders, whether Xhosa, English, or Afrikaans, a bit more propriety is required. Afrikaners greet their elders with the respectful terms *Oom* (uncle) and *Tannie* (aunt), or Mr. and Mrs. You are expected to stand up when elders enter the room, and while these old-fashioned manners may be dying out in the West, they're still evident in traditional Afrikaner families and conservative homes.

When meeting tribal leaders, keep your head lower than theirs, and bow slightly upon entering the room.

DRESS CODE

Generally South Africans are fairly relaxed about dress; however, there are times when visitors are advised to exercise restraint. When visiting religious or cultural centers it is best to dress demurely: low necklines or high-cropped shorts are not appropriate. Bare-breasted women can be seen in many traditional dance routines, but this is a cultural norm, and should not be considered an erotic display.

People naturally dress according to the type of work they do. If out of doors, it is usually protective outdoor clothing; if in an office then "business-casual" is most likely, and sometimes suits. South African summers aren't conducive to restrictive, formal clothing, but suits are required in formal situations.

"Smart-casual dress" is often stated on invitations. This means semi-formal: not a suit, and not flip-flops, but neat, stylish leisurewear.

PERSONAL SPACE AND PRIVACY

Much as South Africans enjoy interaction and socializing, white South Africans are very particular about maintaining "body space." Don't stand too close, and leave a couple of feet of unoccupied space around them. Their black counterparts, on the other hand, have been so used to living at close quarters that this is almost a foreign concept to them.

In terms of information, privacy is guarded in South Africa. The right to privacy is guaranteed in the constitution—that is, people have the right not to have their person, home, or property searched, their possessions seized, or the privacy of their communications violated. Health care is particularly sensitive, in terms of how medical staff counsel and care for HIV/AIDS patients.

EXPRESSION

Some black South Africans express themselves vigorously and physically. They may speak more loudly than you are used to, and this is particularly noticeable in the townships, where people standing a couple of feet apart will think nothing of conducting their conversation at full pitch. Some locals say this is because if they spoke quietly others might think they were gossiping, so it's best to make sure everyone can hear what you're saying. Other people are very expansive with their hand gestures or body movements when emphasizing a point.

Your natural way of expressing yourself will usually be accepted—allowances will made for your foreignness. Be careful not to show any interest or warmth toward other people's children that could be misinterpreted. It's a matter of boundaries. Straightforward friendliness and interest are of course welcomed.

HOSPITALITY

South Africans are hospitable, and love to socialize with friends and family. If you're invited home for a *braai* (barbecue) or a formal dinner, arrive on time. Some occasions are "BYOB" (bring your own bottle/booze) or "bring and *braai*," in which case you're expected to contribute your share of drinks, meat, salads, or other dishes. It's best to ask in advance exactly what you're expected to bring. If your host is vague, then bring meat and drinks at the least, and perhaps a snack to share beforehand—South African gatherings are notorious for serving a meal well into the afternoon or evening after normal eating hours. Even if you are providing your own food and drink, it's still a nice gesture to bring a bottle for your host and flowers or chocolates for your hostess.

The *Braai*

Cooking over the coals is South Africa's national pastime. *Braais* are informal gatherings where families

and friends get together around an open fire, and this can be in one of the many parks, at the beach, in the bushveld, or most often at home. South Africans don't need an excuse for a *braai*.

"*Ons gaan nou braai*" is a phrase that means "We're going to barbecue now" and has become a standing joke in South Africa, since you're likely to hear it from the time you arrive until the meat, finally, gets on to the grill. "Now" could mean in five minutes or five hours. Hence the desirability of bringing snacks for everyone to share until the meat is ready.

A *braai* usually lasts as long as the conversation and the drink flow. It's a time for chatting, laughing, discussing everything (especially politics), and of course eating—eventually.

The Return Match

If you would like to reciprocate, you can invite friends either to your home, if you're a resident, or to a restaurant. If you invite them out, you are expected to pay. They may offer to split the bill, but it's bad form to accept this if you've extended the invitation.

A GUEST IN THE HOUSE

South Africans go out of their way to make newcomers feel welcome, and this may include being invited to stay in their homes. If you're invited to stay, there are a few observances that should make your visit comfortable for everyone. Make sure that you keep your room tidy; even if there is a housekeeper, don't take advantage of it. Offer to help with chores, even if there is domestic help. Offer to cook a meal; some people appreciate someone else taking over the kitchen once in a while. Although the original invitation might have been to "stay as long as you like," be perceptive and gauge how your presence is affecting your hosts. Don't overstay your welcome.

GIFTS

Whether you are going to dinner or accepting a long-weekend invitation, it is both polite and friendly to bring your hosts a gift. South Africa's communities are so diverse that it's difficult to generalize about gift giving, but there are a few guidelines. South Africans typically give presents on birthdays, engagements, and weddings, and at baptism, confirmation, Christmas, Eid, and Hanukkah. When lavish parties are held to celebrate milestone birthdays, the presents should be commensurate, and should always be wrapped. They may be opened when received, or they may be opened later; there's no hard and fast rule.

In some black communities, it is usual to give clothes at Christmas. In poorer communities the most basic necessities are appreciated—soap, candles, and clothes for adults, and stationery or, if possible, school clothing for children. But that doesn't mean that a toy wouldn't be enthusiastically received. Don't expect to receive a gift in return.

DATING

Dating is acceptable in all but the most religious of families. South African children generally start dating in high school or in college, depending on what is acceptable in their community.

The legal age of consent is complex. Although a child legally becomes an adult at the age of eighteen, the age of consent is sixteen. Exceptions apply, for example sex with mentally disabled people. The act of sex must be consensual. Consent for sex above the age of twelve is allowed if the age difference is not more than two years, so a fourteen-year-old and a sixteen-year-old can have consensual sex. It is illegal to have sex with a child under twelve years old. Despite the law condoning sex at this young age, many communities, black and white, completely reject sexual relations at such a tender age.

Interracial relationships are seen as normal and acceptable. Of course there are extremists at both ends of the color spectrum who reject interracial relationships, but they are the exception, not the norm.

Very religious families may still require a courting couple to be chaperoned, but generally when young people start dating they are free to conduct their relationship without interference. Most couples date for about two years before separating, moving in together, or tying the knot. In some traditional African families, the elders, in conjunction with the parents, must give their permission for the couple to date, and in other traditional communities "virginity tests" are done to ensure that young women remain chaste before marriage. Traditionally, the Zulu Reed Dance participants are supposed to be virgins, but this is unlikely in a modern society.

If you date a South African, treat your partner as you would in your home country. If your dating etiquette doesn't match their ideas, you'll soon find out, as they will let you know what they expect from a relationship. Bear in mind that historically, and to a large degree currently, South Africa is a patriarchal society, so traditional women who haven't been fully emancipated will date a man with the intention of pleasing him. However, urban women are less likely to be submissive, and will expect an equal relationship.

If a man invites a woman on a date, he is expected to pay. If a woman wants to pay her share, she'll let him know.

White men, especially foreigners, are much sought after by young black women, since they are perceived to have money and to treat women well, even though black men can and do treat women equally well. Many of these women frequent the upscale hotels and malls looking for company. Be wary, and try to establish whether it is your sparkling wit or your bulging wallet that is the focus of attention.

South Africa has one of the highest HIV/AIDS rates in the world, and it's wise to keep this in mind when deciding to take a relationship further. Testing and screening for STDs can be carried out by any of the health clinics or doctors in the suburbs.

Female sex tourism is fast creeping into Cape Town, and female tourists can be seen hanging on to the arms of their holiday "Rastas" at bars and nightclubs in Long Street, Greenpoint, and Sea Point.

SEXUAL FAVORS

When so many in the country are extremely poor, unequal, predatory relationships are often created in which individuals abuse their positions of power for advancement or gratification. While the granting of political favors is rampant, "social favors" are becoming more evident in South African society.

"Blessers" are usually wealthy businessmen who drive flashy cars and live in prestigious apartment blocks in the chic suburbs, and who buy the favors of attractive young women by paying for their, or their siblings', school fees, or by buying them a pair of high-heeled shoes, a manicure, or cell phone airtime vouchers. Some may call this prostitution, and it's most certainly commercial sexual exploitation.

SOUTH AFRICANS AT HOME

HOUSING

The great disparity in how South Africans live is apparent throughout the country. From towering inner-city apartment blocks to wood, grass, and mud huts in the rural Transkei, from luxurious mansions in the exclusive coastal enclaves to the squatter camps on the edges of the cities, living conditions reflect the extremes of wealth and poverty.

Most black households consist of more than one generation. It is usual in both rural and urban areas for a modest two-roomed house to accommodate grandparents, two or more parents or other adult family members, and several children. This is because family circumstances change regularly and members

take their responsibility to the extended family seriously.
If someone loses their job, it is not unusual for them
to move in with a sibling or parent until the situation
improves. A kitchen by day will be a bedroom by night;
the number of people who can be accommodated is
limited only by the size of the kitchen floor. This is
the reality of life for hundreds of thousands of South
Africans, and it is possible that the young man or woman
who checks out your groceries at the mall or serves your
table at a restaurant is supporting an extended family.

Some Muslim Indian families may also consist
of grandparents, sons and daughters-in-law, and
grandchildren. This is changing, and today many South
African Muslim Indians prefer to live in nuclear family
units, like their Hindu and Tamil counterparts.

Far from the foreign stereotype, not all white South
Africans are rich. During apartheid, many poor white
workers were pulled out of poverty and given basic
jobs. Since 1994, many have suffered as employment
legislation has swung toward protecting the black
majority. For the first time since the Depression of
the 1930s, significant numbers of blue-collar white
South Africans are unemployed, and some now live, as
hundreds of thousands of their black compatriots do, in
shantytowns known as "informal settlements." However,

to say that this is the norm or a growing trend would be misleading, and most whites live in pleasant, leafy suburbs—whether in lower-middle-class mixed-race areas or exclusive upper-class areas.

A growing trend since 1994 has been for destitute people to move into inner-city apartments or commercial blocks that have been vacated by their owners. These buildings are considered "hijacked," and their electrical and water connections are usually illegal, a drain on the cities' resources, and very dangerous. Most of the illegal connections involve live wires that are merely covered by a carpet, and hundreds of people die every year trying to appropriate electricity. or stepping on a live wire. Trash is usually dumped out of windows, creating severe health hazards—rat poison is a fast-moving line for vendors in the inner cities and townships. Many multinationals have moved their headquarters to new commercial hubs in the suburbs, such as Sandton in Johannesburg. There have been attempts to revitalize and rennovate the inner cities, but these are mainly funded by the private sector and receive no more than lip service from local government.

At the opposite end of the spectrum, there are gated, high-security property developments with controlled access that could rival a maximum security prison. In these estates, families enjoy a semblance of normalcy and peace of mind that is difficult to achieve in the ordinary suburbs, where opportunist criminals prey on unsuspecting victims. One such development is Steyn City, a 800-hectare (nearly 2,000-acre) estate between Johannesburg and Pretoria, a stone's throw away from the most desperate of informal settlements, Diepsloot, which has no roads, no formal lighting, no running water, and no sewage system; it is just one tin shack built upon another. Fires break out every week and emergency services are unable to reach them because of the narrow walkways. It is this kind of incongruity that inflames the feeling that meaningful economic transformation has not been achieved.

DAILY LIFE

Early morning in the affluent suburbs sees any number of runners, walkers, and cyclists getting their daily exercise fix before rushing off to their nine-to-five jobs. The gym parking lots are also usually full in the hours before 9:00 a.m. and after 4:00 p.m.

Poor South Africans have a completely different reality. They are usually up well before dawn (4:00 a.m.) to prepare their families for the day before starting the long trek to work. The black townships were always built far from the major cities, and the spatial planning has not fundamentally changed. Property developers continue to build affordable housing on the outskirts of the city or near black townships where the land is cheaper and they can make better profits.

The people who live in these communities have to travel far, and take at least an hour to reach their places of work. Women who walk in the dark to get to the taxi stands or bus stations are exposed to crime and rape. The taxis are often overloaded and ignore the rules of the road, putting the lives of their passengers in danger, but passengers are too afraid to demand that they drive safely. They are often involved in horrific motor accidents. Most people traveling into the cities and suburbs have to take two or more taxis to reach their places of employment, and transportation costs are a large portion of their monthly budget.

Johannesburg and Cape Town have built rapid transportation systems, and Durban is in the process of rolling out its schemes, but it is still costly for ordinary people to use public transportation.

Most people work from nine to five, but South Africa is gaining a reputation for having an informal four-and-a-half-day week in the corporate sector. On a Friday, many white-collar employees organize working lunches and simply don't return to the office, which has had an impact on productivity. On the other hand, some blue-collar workers are notorious for taking Mondays off, usually after a weekend of fun and alcohol.

School hours are usually 7:45 a.m. to 1:45 p.m., and many schools have cultural or sporting activities in the afternoons. Popular school sports are soccer, rugby, basketball, cricket, netball, and swimming. Most suburban schools have after-school facilities for children whose parents work a full day. Here they have a place to do supervised homework and some form of sport or play time with their friends. In the townships, however, lack of finances and facilities means that in the afternoons young children play in the streets with their friends, usually only casually supervised.

South Africans generally head home after work during the week and spend time with their families, or watch television. Crime has played a part in stopping people from walking around the suburbs. White people drive everywhere, whether it's to the corner café or the mall, while their black counterparts in the townships usually walk, or take a taxi if it is too far.

Most families try to have meals together, but with many parents leaving for work before dawn and returning long after sunset this isn't always possible. Families fortunate enough to have a parent or a housekeeper to do the cooking can usually enjoy some meals together around the table. South Africans range from fast-food fanatics to the very health conscious.

WEEKENDS

South Africans like to get out on weekends. Many suburbanites go to the popular inner-city markets where they can enjoy food from all over the world in a festive atmosphere, and where they can browse the upscale craft stalls for pricey handicrafts such as hand-embroidered linen, custom-made pottery, and gourmet vinegars. Others escape the madness of the working week by heading for their houses on the river or coast, or to the bushveld. Yet others stay put and take the opportunity for a two-day rest.

The bush (countryside) is usually within an hour's drive of several of South Africa's major cities, and the wonderful climate and abundance of natural beauty mean that people can spend a lot of time enjoying it.

Social media has opened up access to communities of like-minded people, and young people with similar interests connect on Instagram or Facebook and get together in major cities to enjoy photography, hiking, birdwatching, indoor soccer, art gallery browsing, or whatever takes their fancy. However they are spent, weekends are casual, and South Africans take full advantage of their leisure activities.

On Fridays some Indian stores shut down just before lunchtime so that their owners can attend prayers at the mosques. On Friday evenings ultra-Orthodox Jewish families step out together to the synagogue, and again on Saturday mornings. On Saturday nights and Sunday mornings, black Christians flock to their places of worship. If you live near a nature reserve in the city or the beach, it is likely that you'll see small groups of worshipers dressed in long robes gathered in the open air, some praying loudly, others just quietly going about their rituals. In South Africa the right to worship is respected.

DOMESTIC STAFF

Many South Africans who live in the suburbs have housekeepers and gardeners. These employees may live on or off the property, and it is usual to pay them more if they live out to cover transportation costs. By international standards, the wages paid to domestic employees are very low, even though there is a statutory minimum wage. In 2016, it was between R2,200 and R2,400 per month, depending on whether they worked in a metropolitan or a rural area. Either way, the wage only allows for basic subsistence. Employees who live on their employer's property are usually given meals and take Thursday afternoons off, while weekend work is negotiable. Most domestic workers don't work on Sundays. Thursday night is when suburbanites traditionally go out for dinner, so it's advisable to reserve a table on this night as well as on the weekend.

SHOPPING

Some of the weekend is taken up with shopping, since it may be the only time working people have a chance to replenish supplies or just enjoy a bit of retail therapy. There are malls in the suburbs and the townships, with shops that cater to the specific demographics of each community, and the major international brands—food and retail—are all present. Shopping for groceries and clothing is usually a family affair, with children in tow.

Some people make a whole day of a trip to the mall. They shop, eat, watch a movie, go bowling, and meet friends. Others like to meet friends or family in one of the fashionable districts in the CBD—the Central Business District—and have a prolonged meal together.

All the major chain stores offer an online service, and deliveries are prompt.

CAR GUARDS

When you park your car in a parking bay on a commercial street, you'll probably be greeted by someone in a bright yellow or orange bib. These self-appointed guards are alerting you to the fact that they'll be looking after your car while you go about your business. Their presence may put off any opportunistic criminals, but it is no guarantee. However, on your return you will be expected to cough up a few Rand to the car guard, who will ensure that you can exit the parking bay safely into the traffic. These car guards are predominantly migrants from the Democratic Republic of Congo, many of whom are highly educated; but lack of language and qualification accreditation prevents them from being employed in the formal sector. Often, when they arrive or leave for duty in any number, they sing songs from their homeland, and it's quite a moving performance.

GROWING UP IN SOUTH AFRICA

Children are cherished in all of South Africa's family-oriented cultures. Nevertheless, while it is illegal to smack a child, there are some very Calvinistic communities that believe in "spare the rod and spoil the child." For the most part, children are well behaved and happy, and parents, as anywhere in the world, want to do what's best for them.

While children are considered a blessing, in black communities they are also an insurance policy, so parents invest everything they have in their children to equip them for a life that will enable them to look after their parents in old age. Residential retirement homes

or retirement villages are not favored by black families, who think it's a family's responsibility to look after their elderly; however, many state retirement homes now have black residents—a sign that times have changed and the extended family isn't always the norm in urban areas.

In any community, there are children who fall through the cracks, who, for whatever reason, have to make their own way in the world. South African children who have been abandoned are incredibly resourceful, and will use whatever skills they have to put on a performance at traffic lights to earn a few Rand to buy food, or very possibly to feed a drug habit. Nyaope is the drug of choice for many homeless or neglected youngsters. Manufactured from a mix of anti-retrovirals and heroin, it is a scourge in South African society.

In the townships children grow up very quickly. It's a survive-or-die world, and from a young age township children are expected to entertain themselves and look after each other. If their parents work away from home and are absent for long hours, and there is no adult supervision, they are expected to fend for themselves.

Upper-middle class suburban children have a very different experience. They are provided with everything they need, and generally protected from the dark side of life. There are enormous disparities between the two groups. Township children are usually able to get on with children from all walks of life because they are used to dealing with members of a mixed society, while upper-middle-class children are insulated from poverty and other social ills, and it is usually only through their school's social responsibility programs that they come into contact with people from other walks of life, albeit in a staged setting. Many schools in the suburbs have outreach programs, usually in the city center rather than in the heart of the townships or informal settlements—understandably, since there is risk.

EDUCATION
Education, as we have seen, is prized by most South Africans, and each generation seeks to improve their children's educational prospects.

Everything in South Africa is affected by the past, and no sector continues to be as disadvantaged as education for black people. When the education system was racially segregated, the provision for blacks was deliberately inferior. Since 1994 progress has been made in applying a single syllabus, but the reality is that black schools still don't have the resources to raise standards. Many children drop out at the end of primary school, and many more before the end of high school. In interviews, the reasons they give are mainly financial, and then poor academic performance, which discourages them from continuing. Those who do graduate have often been poorly taught and lack the skills or expertise to go to college or enter the workplace. Some may never manage to get a job.

While the central government provides the national framework for school policy, the provinces are responsible for administering it. School governing bodies have a say in the running of schools. Private schools and higher education institutions have a fair amount of autonomy, but must adhere to government policies, such as not excluding a child on the grounds of race or religion. The government runs a food program in the poorer areas where often the meal children receive at school is their only square meal of the day.

There are three official education sectors, namely General Education and Training, Further Education and Training (FET), and Higher Education and Training.

General education spans thirteen years from Grade 0, or Grade R (reception), through to Grade 12, or matric, as it is commonly referred to. School is compulsory for all children from the ages of seven to fifteen, or the completion of Grade 9. FET takes place from Grades 10 to 12, and includes career-oriented training that takes place in other FET colleges. Diplomas and certificates are awarded at this level. General Education and Training includes Adult Basic Education and Training (ABET), which is available to adults who wish to complete their basic education.

Young people doing City and Guild (vocational) courses in South African technical schools often aren't awarded their certificates because they have not been able to fulfill the practical parts of their courses. Many colleges have inferior or even no equipment, and much of the training is purely theoretical, which means that employers are unwilling to take students on because they don't have practical experience. Sometimes companies and individuals who are willing to employ them aren't formally registered as businesses, and so are not accredited to provide on-the-job training. This causes dissatisfaction all around—from parents who have paid a fortune for education, to dissatisfied employers, and ultimately disillusioned graduates.

South Africa has twenty-three state-funded higher education institutions, including universities and technology institutes. While the state subsidizes tuition fees at these institutions, students often have to pay the balance of the fees as well as board and lodgings. In the last few decades South African universities have been a magnet for international students, both for the quality of education and because of the competitive fees, relative to other countries. However, there have been continuous student protests under the slogan #FeesMustFall. Negotiations between university administrators and students are ongoing, and violence has erupted both on and off campus as students and police have clashed. The government has remained relatively removed from these discussions, despite the fact that the ANC initiated the suggestion of free higher education.

South Africa's average student reading score places it tenth out of fifteen African countries, and its average mathematics score places it eighth in the same group. The adult literacy rate is 93.7 percent in adults more than twenty years of age (2015). It is broadly acknowledged that in a country with a skills shortage a solution to unaffordable university fees will have to be found.

chapter six

TIME OUT

South Africans are able to spend a lot of time out of doors thanks to the excellent weather. They are inclined to take lots of small breaks and work out their holiday times to coincide with public holidays and weekends to get the maximum time off. They aren't put off by long distances, and think nothing of traveling six hours to

a family wedding or to spend a weekend in the mountains. They just load up the car and head out.

There are plenty of outdoor leisure activities—all kinds of sports, park concerts, or soccer matches to watch at the many impressive stadiums around the country. All tastes are catered to, from outdoor theatrical performances to hikes to Cape Point, where the Atlantic and Indian Oceans meet.

SOUTH AFRICAN CUISINE

South Africa is a culinary melting pot and a foodie's paradise. Its diverse culture is reflected in the many different styles of cooking, and you would be hard pressed to name an international cuisine that can't be found in the major cities. Good-quality local produce is abundant and the current trend of artisanal food has resulted in the growing of a wide variety of exotic fruits and vegetables. The legendary wine route in the Western Cape offers a great culinary and wine-tasting experience. Most wine estates have restaurants with food and wine pairings to showcase the local fare.

South Africans are big meat eaters. Meat is the staple of almost every meal for those who can afford it, and local red meat is particularly flavorful. In black townships the smell of roasting *chisa nyama* (hot meat) wafts on the air. This barbecued meat, which ranges from goat to beef and usually includes a slab of the cheaper cuts, is commonly accompanied by side dishes of chopped tomato, onion, and coleslaw, and *chakalaka* or *seshebo*, which is a tomato, onion, and chili relish.

In African and Afrikaans homes you're likely to be served chicken or beef accompanied by *pap—mieliepap*, or maize meal—which is still the staple

diet of most black people and also popular with
Afrikaners. *Mieliepap* can be served as a soft porridge,
or as *stywepap*, which has a stiff, breadlike consistency,
and which one breaks off in pieces and dunks into
stews, or eats as an accompaniment to meals. *Marog*
(amaranth) is a spinach-like vegetable that grows wild,
and one often sees women picking it from vacant plots
of urban ground. In the townships you may come across
"smileys"—boiled sheep heads—or "walkie-talkies"—
chicken feet and heads. A popular African delicacy in
the northern part of the country is the mopani worm,
a small caterpillar that lives on the mopani tree. It is
usually sun-dried for use later, or may be barbecued.

Bobotie is a traditional Cape Malay dish of beef
or lamb mince, nuts, and chutney, baked in an egg
custard. Other traditional Cape Malay dishes are *Malay
koeksusters*, which are spicy fried dough balls sprinkled
with coconut (not to be confused with the Afrikaans
koeksusters, which are plaited dough, cooked, and
steeped in syrup); *bredies*, which are spicy lamb and beef
stews; and *gesmoorde vis*, which is braised fish.

Local Indian food is spicy and aromatic. Typically it
consists of spicy curries accompanied by *sambals* and
raita. Bunny chow is an authentic South African Indian
favorite. It is a loaf of white bread cut in half; the soft
center is removed and retained, and the loaf shell is filled
with curry. The removed bread is eaten dipped into the
curry, and then the shell itself, infused with the curry
sauce, is devoured. *Biryani* is an oven-baked, highly
spiced saffron rice dish that usually contains meat,
vegetables, and fried potatoes. *Samoosas* are triangular
fried pastries with savory meat or vegetable fillings.

If asked to describe what kind of food they prefer,
Afrikaners might say, "I'm a *vleis, rys, en patat* (meat,
rice, and potato) person." This probably goes back to the

days when they were farmers and needed the sustenance of protein and starch. *Boerewors* is a traditional, highly spiced, coarse sausage, usually cooked on the *braai*. There's no one recipe for it, since every sausage maker has a "secret family recipe," but a commonly enjoyed *boerewors* is the Grabouw variety, which has strong hints of roasted coriander.

Traditionally, Afrikaners like their vegetables to be dressed, such as pumpkin tossed in butter and cinnamon, or green beans mixed with onion and a little puréed potato. It is also common for them to use jam as a condiment with their meat dinners. *Vetkoek*, a doughnut with savory filling, and *koeksusters* are favorite dough-based treats. *Melktert*, a custard milk tart with cinnamon, and Cape Brandy Tart, or "Tipsy Tart," are local traditional desserts worth sampling. *Biltong* is dried, salted, spiced beef or game, which tastes quite different from American jerky.

To get a real taste of South Africa, visitors should sample food from far and wide.

AND TO WASH IT DOWN
Akubekuhle! *Gesondheid*! Cheers! Except for certain religious communities, South Africans are the biggest social drinkers in Africa. Alcohol is the most popular

social lubricant. Young working people may meet friends for a drink after work, go on a pub crawl to celebrate a groom's final hours as a single man, or party on a booze cruise on the Vaal River or at Durban Harbour.

South Africa has been producing wine since the

eighteenth century. Its signature grape variety, Pinotage, a cross between Pinot Noir and Cinsaut, has become a symbol of its distinctive winemaking tradition. For wine-lovers, a leisurely tasting tour of the beautiful Cape Winelands is a must. There are also some uniquely South African spirits and aperitifs, as well as fortified wines such as sherries and ports.

South Africans are great lager drinkers, and can choose from most of the international brands and well-established local brews such as Black Label (known in the townships as Zamalek), Castle, and Windhoek. Craft beers that make regular appearances at festivals and craft markets are also popular, although they are more expensive than the commercial brands. The cheaper, native sorghum beer favored by some black people is a thick, milky brew sold in cartons, and is quite palatable to the Western tongue.

Most cultural tours to black townships include a trip to a *shebeen*. During the apartheid era *shebeens* were illegal drinking dens where black people, barred from entering white pubs and bars, could socialize. They were usually run by "Shebeen Queens," women who sold home-brewed alcohol in a relaxed and friendly environment. The *shebeens* played an important role in black communities, providing a place where activists and community members could express themselves both politically and culturally. It was the *shebeens* that helped give rise to the *kwaito*, a slowed-down garage or house music. *Shebeens* continue to be places where patrons meet and have *chisa nyama* and a bottle of brew and maybe a bit of dancing. They are now mainly owned by men.

Cafés and restaurants are open all week, but tend to be quiet until Thursday, Friday, and weekend evenings. In line with the international coffee-drinking trend there is a growing community of coffee *aficionados*, and while chains such as Starbucks have joined the scene there are many independent cafés worth visiting simply to sample their house blends. Ethiopian coffee *baristas* can be found at most inner-city markets, whose preparation ritual is as much an experience as the flavor of the coffee.

EATING OUT

Depending on whether you're looking for a leisurely dinner or a quick snack, there are eating establishments to suit. Street food really only exists in the townships and in inner-city areas near the transport hubs. Most street vendors sell fruit and light snacks such as peanuts and potato chips, while a few sell grilled corn or meat and chicken stews and *pap*. They cater mostly to workers looking for something to eat on the go.

Many restaurants are large chain franchises, but there are plenty of independent niche restaurants or just old family favorites with loyal customers. Burger King came to South Africa in 2013, but lovers of the Ultimate Bacon Cheeseburger be warned: the franchise is *halal* (conforms to Islamic dietary law) and there's no bacon on the menu. If you are entertaining guests or planning a special night out with a good meal and a bottle of wine, always check first whether your chosen restaurant serves alcohol—*halal* establishments do not.

The *Confrérie de la Chaîne des Rôtisseurs*, established by Louis IX in Paris in 1248, is a worldwide association of member chefs, gourmets, and restaurants, of which there are a number in South Africa. Restaurants carrying its blazon and are therefore a good bet. *Chaîne* status covers not only classical French cuisine, but gourmet fare from other cultures too, including South African.

The cost of meat, relative to other countries, is very low, so for visitors a prime steak is surprisingly cheap. Restaurants like the Carnivore in the northern suburbs of Johannesburg offer an impressive menu of game, including springbok, warthog, or crocodile. *Chisa nyame* has now become popular in the suburbs.

Cape Malay cuisine combines African, Malaysian, and Indonesian flavors. It uses a blend of spices—cumin, coriander, cinnamon, ginger, fennel, cardamom, star anise, tamarind, and turmeric—and dried fruit to create piquant stews and curries. Found throughout the Western Cape, it is best sampled in Bo-Kaap, on the lower slopes of Table Mountain.

TIPPING

Tips are expected, and the following is a rough guide.

Restaurants and bars: 10–15 percent is usual, if there is no service charge. For groups of ten or more diners there is usually a service charge of 10 percent.

Parking attendants and security guards: from R2, depending on how long you were gone.

Gas station attendants: anything from R2 if they just pumped gas, or more if they also checked your tire pressure and oil level.

Airport porters: R5–10 per piece of luggage.

Hotel porters: R10–20 per porter service.

Tour guides and drivers: usually a group makes a collection and gives a combined tip. Single travelers can use their discretion.

Roadside vendors, such as newspaper sellers: usually round up the cost of your newspaper.

Hairdressers, beauty salon assistants, and the like are not usually tipped, but the shampooist would be grateful for a R10 tip.

SMOKING

Many foreigners are shocked by South Africa's draconian drinking and smoking laws, but South Africans feel they're a healthier nation because of them. Smoking is prohibited indoors, in partially enclosed public spaces, and in areas and cars where children under the age of twelve are present. Children under the age of eighteen may not purchase cigarettes or enter designated smoking areas. Smoking is also banned on domestic flights, in airport terminals, on public transport, and in cinemas and shopping malls. Some hotels are strictly non-smoking. It's best to ask if smoking is permitted and where you might be allowed to do so. The fine for the owner of any establishment—restaurant or office—that breaks the law is a maximum of R50,000. Individual smokers are fined R500.

NIGHTLIFE

For people looking for a *jol* (good time), there are nightclubs in all the major cities. From the legendary thirty-seven-year-old Club Galaxy in the Mother City (Cape Town) to Taboo in South Africa's richest square mile (Sandton, Johannesburg), there are clubs to suit every taste. You can get down and party to international and local DJs, and there's every possibility that in the high season you can rub shoulders with the likes of Justin Bieber, Santana, and other international celebrities.

The club scene has a strong bouncer culture to keep under-age children and loud revelers out of the nightclubs and to protect their turf, and they're not known for their tact. If approached by a bouncer and asked to leave, don't argue; submit and move on.

GAMBLING

Gambling is legal for people over the age of eighteen, and while horse-racing has declined somewhat since the introduction of the national lottery in 2000, there are still one or two major races, such as the Durban July and the Cape Town Met, where celebrities show off their designer wear.

Casinos are very popular and usually offer more than just gambling. In addition to restaurants, nightclubs, and play areas for children, they often host impressive scientific, historical, and cultural exhibitions that the whole family can enjoy.

Gamblers come from all walks of life. Informal outdoor dice games attract people down on their luck and hoping to hit the big time. On Thursday nights, many domestic workers can be seen slipping coins into the slot machines at one of the city casinos. A thriving industry of pawn shops has sprung up around the casinos where gamblers can pawn everything from their car to their engagement rings or cell phones to get another fistful of money to throw down the dice in the hope that Lady Luck will smile on them.

LIVE ENTERTAINMENT

South Africa has a vibrant performing arts scene and there are theaters in all the major urban centers, including Soweto. The whole gamut of performing arts can be found, from music, song, and dance, to drama, satire, and stand-up comedy.

Music

Music is an essential part of South African life. South Africans make it, move to it, and listen to it. The diverse musical culture includes hip-hop, kwaito, gospel, rock, pop, Afrikaans rap-rave, and jazz— the last, having a long history, is considered struggle music. Much of the contemporary music scene is a mix of African, American, and European music, exemplified by singer and songwriter Simphiwe Dana, who combines jazz, pop,

and traditional music in her repertoire. Kwaito is a uniquely South African genre based on house music beats but characterized by melodic African sounds and vocals, and usually sung by a male singer. The choral group Ladysmith Black Mambazo, trumpeter Hugh Masekela, rap-rave group Die Antwoord, and pianist and composer Abdullah Ibrahim delight international audiences. Other popular groups include Freshlyground, Locnville, Karen Zoid, and Jack Parow.

Today the country hosts many international artists. Foreign fans fly into South Africa to see their musical heroes because it is relatively cheap to do so.

There are three full-time Classical orchestras in South Africa. Cape Town Opera has a year-round program, regularly tours abroad, and conducts workshops around the country. Opera Africa in Sandton was set up specifically to reach new audiences. Multimedia artist William Kentridge has designed and staged operas around the world.

Dance
South African music is steeped in dance culture. Zulu warriors danced on the battlefield, Shebeen Queens boogied in the taverns doing the *pata-pata* (touch-touch) made famous by Miriam Makeba's song of the same name, and political protesters have long done the high-stepping *toyi-toyi* dance as they chant. Since 1994, township dance has flourished as an art, and popular dance culture such as *marabi* and *pantsula* is now performed on stage.

Possibly unexpectedly, ballet is popular, and there are ballet schools across the country nurturing talent from the suburbs to the townships. International prima ballerina Phyllis Spira was born in South Africa. The late John Cranko was a celebrated choreographer with the Royal Ballet and the Stuttgart Ballet.

Theater

From the open-air Shakespeare performances at Maynardville Park in Wynberg, Cape Town, to the challenging plays of Athol Fugard and ground-breaking productions at the Market Theatre in Johannesburg, South African theater has a strong tradition, and today the theater scene is buzzing. Venues range from formal theaters to converted country bars and casinos. The best-attended event is the Annual National Arts Festival held each winter in Grahamstown, which has showcased performing and graphic artists for thirty years, and includes a well-supported fringe theater. John Kani, Athol Fugard, and Lara Foot are notable in the local theater scene, while Janet Suzman and Anthony Sher are South Africa's most famous theatrical exports.

The local film industry is doing well, with a couple of international awards under its belt and exports of actors such as Oscar-winner Charlize Theron.

LITERATURE

South Africa has an impressive literary tradition and boasts two contemporary literary giants—Nobel laureates Nadine Gordimer and J. M. Coetzee. Other writers who achieved international acclaim are Olive Schreiner, Alan Paton, and Laurens van der Post, while contemporary authors Lauren Beukes, Deon Meyer, Zakes Mda, and S. L. Grey are enjoying significant success. South African writers come from diverse backgrounds, and their writing often reflects the pain of past conflicts and present tensions.

MUSEUMS AND GALLERIES

For a fascinating insight into the cultural, political, and social dynamics of the country there are scores of museums dedicated to subjects ranging from aviation to ostrich farming to beer. Each province has its own collections reflecting the local culture and history. The Iziko Museums of South Africa and their associated collections (the word *iziko* is Xhosa for "hearth") are run by the Department of Arts and Culture, and cover science, natural history, social history, art, and anthropology. The Iziko South African National Gallery, in the Dutch East India Company's Garden in Cape Town, has a collection of Dutch, French, and British works from the seventeenth to the nineteenth centuries, including lithographs, etchings, and some early-twentieth-century British paintings. Contemporary art in the gallery is selected from many of South Africa's communities, and there is an authoritative collection of sculpture and beadwork.

Period paintings and artifacts are also on display in historic sites such as Groot Constantia (the colonial Dutch governor's residence) and the gabled Cape

Dutch homes of the Winelands. Near the National Gallery, the Iziko South African Museum houses important exhibitions and displays of African zoology, palaeontology, and archaeology. The Gertrude Posel Gallery at Wits University in Johannesburg and the Durban Art Gallery house works of historical and anthropological significance, such as masks, appliqué cloths, ceremonial aprons, and carved chairs.

The Apartheid Museum in Johannesburg is a moving memorial to the recent past, with impressive interactive dislays.

MONEY

The South African currency is the Rand, and while you might find someone who will accept foreign currency you'd be better off equipping yourself with Rands or using an ATM card. Most credit cards are accepted, although it is worth noting that many stores don't accept American Express, possibly because of the high rate of fraud experienced with that card. ATMs are available on almost every corner. However, be very

cautious when drawing cash, since ATM fraud is a
major problem (see page 145).

"Robot Hustlers" and Beggars

Sometimes it seems as though you can't drive a
hundred meters without being accosted by a beggar
or a "robot hustler." These are people who stand at the
traffic lights (called "robots" in South Africa) who are
either brandishing a cardboard sign to try to get you
to part with R10 or R20, or who want to sell you cheap
goods from China. Either way, they can be persistent,
and even aggressive if they are not given money or
allowed to wash your windshield. It's best to keep the
windows closed and not to engage in conversation
with them. Very often they are substance abusers who
need the money to fuel their habit. Some beggars
are genuinely needy, but most civic and religious
organizations provide feeding schemes and urge
motorists not to support the hustlers.

SHOPPING FOR PLEASURE

Die-hard shoppers are well catered to in the malls. All
the leading international brands can be found there,
and there are many local brands, from Mr. Price to
Black Coffee, to encourage shoppers to spend their
money. The Mall of Africa, situated between Tshwane
and Johannesburg, is the largest mall in the southern
hemisphere, and the scenic V&A Waterfront on Table
Bay and the Gateway shopping center on the northern
KZN coast are popular shopping destinations.

Many local fashion designers have incorporated
African design into their clothing brands and are
creating fashion brands that are sought after, such as
Black Coffee and MapsXSpree.

Art and Handicrafts

South Africa's artistic heritage encompasses prehistoric rock art, figurative African sculpture, colonial representational painting, modern international influences, and the work of contemporary artists inspired by the recent and deeper past. Today there is a vibrant and sophisticated art scene. The works of Irma Stern, Tinus de Jongh, Gerard Sekoto, Wally Serote, and William Kentridge, to name but a few, feature regularly at international auction houses. South  African art continues to reach international galleries.

A wide variety of arts and crafts are produced in studios, on city sidewalks, and in rural areas. Traditional artifacts are made from beads, grass, leather, fabric, and clay, but today the repertoire includes materials that would normally be discarded—gas cans, wire, bottle tops, tin cans, labels from food jars and cans, and plastic bags. These are used to great effect for decorative bric-a-brac and trinkets. The white wood of jacaranda trees, which are not indigenous and therefore not protected, has become popular for carvings. Traditional embroiderers create beautiful linen and tableware, sometimes incorporating beadwork. Local crafters are constantly creating new designs and products.

In addition to the shops and markets, there are African art and craft collectives that provide employment and income for communities, such as the basketry initiative in Fugitive's Drift in KZN, and the project with displaced San people of the Northern Cape Schmidtsdrift community, who produce paintings modeled on the ancient rock art of their ancestors.

Basketry can be found both in rural homes and on display in fine galleries.

Ndebele artist Esther Mahlangu has adapted the distinctive, highly colored geometric Ndebele designs

usually applied to houses to everything from cars to airplanes. The Ndebele style has been extended beautifully to beadwork, which was traditionally the insignia of tribal royalty. It now covers everything from matchboxes to the reproduction traditional small beadwork brooches known as Zulu love letters.

The African Craft Market in Rosebank, Johannesburg, is one of the few places in the world where you can see a vast range of African arts and crafts, whether they be masks, carved chairs, or embroidered or appliqué cloth.

South African folk art has made inroads into the European and American markets. The ceramicist Bonnie Ntshalinsthali's traditional African pottery is represented in major collections in South Africa, Great Britain, and the US. Chickenman Mkize made mock road signs out of cheap materials, and decorated them with eccentric messages. Mkize was illiterate, and transcribed words written out by others with random spacing, adding to the charm of his works, such as "NODRUNK ENBUMS" and "BUTISI TART?"

One of the major exporters of South African arts and crafts is the fast-food franchise Nandos, which allows only South African art and decorations to be displayed in its international outlets.

Wherever you travel, children will eagerly approach you with their handmade wares, from delicate wire cars that actually move, to clay animals, and a catapult made from a branch and a bit of leather.

SPORTS AND FITNESS

South Africa is a sporting nation and fitness ranks high. Wherever you travel you'll come across fitness centers, joggers crossing busy intersections, cyclists on the suburban roads in the early morning, and athletes warming up on sports fields or dusty urban roads.

Sports are akin to religion here. Everything from the CrossFit physical fitness trend to dragon boat racing is on offer. On weekends there are usually national and sometimes international cricket, soccer, or rugby matches, but even soccer pitches in dusty Karoo towns are places to gather to cheer on the local team.

Today by far the most popular sport is soccer, and local teams such as Kaiser Chiefs and Orlando Pirates are supported more strongly than the national team, Bafana Bafana. Black schoolchildren usually play soccer, while most Afrikaans and some English schools favor rugby, although both sports are usually offered in suburban schools. Because of its apartheid-era roots, rugby has a stronger infrastructure, with clubs, leagues, and championships, but it can't shake off the connotation of being a "white" sport, in spite of the attempts to eradicate race in all sport. The national sporting teams are Bafana Bafana, the soccer team, the rugby team known as Amabokke (formerly the Springboks), and the cricket team, the Proteas.

During apartheid times South Africa was a sporting pariah, and wasn't allowed to compete in the international arena. Today South African athletes perform in all international fixtures, but the government has expressed disappointment with the lack of transformation in sports at the club, provincial, and national levels, and blames the administrators for failing to ensure that teams are demographically representative. In spite of the fact that the World Cup funds didn't quite find their way to needy soccer enthusiasts, the government has clamped down on hosting international fixtures in rugby, cricket, athletics, and netball until real transformation has taken place.

There are CrossFit gyms in almost every town. CrossFit is a natural fitness system that uses traditional weights and methods, rather than the machine-oriented environment of many modern fitness centers.

OUT AND ABOUT

There are places to suit all holidaymakers. Some head for budget-beating caravan or camping sites, while others live it up in style at exclusive bush, beach, or golf resorts that only the super-rich can enjoy.

The major rivers are used for leisure activities such as fishing, canoeing, whitewater rafting, sailing, water skiing, and rowing. Some people have holiday homes on the banks of rivers or dams, and spend weekends there with family and friends.

South Africa boasts some of the finest beaches in the world, among them thirty-one high-quality Blue Flag beaches. The warm Indian Ocean on the east coast keeps beach lovers coming back for super surfing, swimming, and sunbathing. Umhlanga in KZN has a holiday vibe all year round, and Durban's Golden Mile is a beach attraction as well as home to top hotels, bars, and nightclubs. Most major beaches are manned by lifeguards and have shark nets. If there are no guards on duty, be sure to swim only between the beacons. It's not advisable to swim at dusk.

The beaches on the Atlantic Ocean are no less lovely; some of the most famous are Clifton and Sandy Bay, South Africa's only nudist beach, near Llandudno, on the western coast of the Cape Peninsula. At Boulders Beach on the eastern side near Simon's Town, swimmers are protected from the winds by the huge granite boulders and joined by African penguins.

"Cultural villages" have been established in most provinces to offer visitors an insight into the traditional culture of the area. There is usually a guided walkabout, a presentation by a guide, or by video, and a song and dance show. There is generally a craft or curio center where you can buy arts and crafts made by the community or representative of its culture. Some impromptu village "malls" spring up on roadsides near semi-rural townships where you can buy local wares and produce, from unbaked clay animal sculptures in the Drakensberg, to bullwhips in Harrismith, and bananas or fresh crayfish on the KZN south coast.

WILDLIFE

Famous for the Big Five—elephant, rhino, buffalo, lion, and leopard—South Africa has wildlife in abundance, despite serious issues with poaching. There are nineteen National Parks representing several different biomes, the largest of which is the Kruger, and

hundreds of provincial, regional, local, and municipal parks. Game lodges abound, and can be found within an hour's drive from many major cities. You can arrange commercial safaris ranging from walking with lions to sleeping in tented camps under the stars while listening to elephants foraging nearby.

For something different, the annual frog night is held in December in the lake district of Chrissiesmeer in the western Free State. You will be taught how to catch, tag, and release frogs, which "sing" all the while!

South Africa is an attractive birding destination. Habitats include wetlands, riverine bush, woodland, desert, and the ocean, and are home to more than 900 bird species. Many enthusiasts come to see the endemic species, such as the blue crane (South Africa's national bird), the black oystercatcher, and the Cape vulture. In the suburbs it's common to be woken by the cry of the noisy mini pterodactyl, the hadeda ibis, that feeds around the edges of suburban gardens.

ORGANIZED TOURS

Even if you're visiting only one of the country's vast provinces you're bound to experience something unique and breathtaking. There are many ASATA-registered travel operators who can advise you on reputable tour organizers. There are also smaller operators who arrange tailored tours to areas that usually include home visits, and if you would like to get a taste of local life, they can offer a more intimate look at South African lifestyles. It's best to go in a group.

The Red Bus Tours that operate in all the world's major cities are available in South Africa's big cities too, and an audio-guided bus tour is a great introduction to what the city has to offer.

SOME MAJOR HIGHLIGHTS

Gauteng	Constitutional Hill in Johannesburg, the site of a former prison and military fort, is now the country's Constitutional Court. It is a living museum that tells the story of South Africa's turbulent past and its journey to democracy.
	Apartheid Museum, Johannesburg
Limpopo	Kruger National Park
Mpumalanga	God's Window, the view from the Drakensberg escarpment
	Bourke's Luck Potholes, outside Graskop. A series of geological formations made up of interconnected pools interlinked with sandstone outcrops
North West	The 27-mile (45-km) Taung Heritage Route allows visitors a glimpse into the journey of our hominid ancestors and the area where early humans lived. It includes the Taung skull discovery site.
Free State	The Golden Gate Highlands National Park has vast open spaces and grassland. Bushmen paintings can be seen in the caves.
Western Cape	Table Mountain and Cape Point form part of the Table Mountain National Park, which stretches from Signal Hill to Cape Point and the Cape Peninsula coastlines.
	Cape Point is a narrow band of land between the Atlantic and the Indian Oceans. It has beautiful bays, beaches, and valleys that are home to diverse and unique flora and fauna.
Eastern Cape	The Addo Elephant National Park has the densest African elephant population in the world. It is the only nature reserve that hosts Africa's Big Seven—elephant, rhino, lion, buffalo, leopard, southern right whale, and the great white shark.
Northern Cape	The Karoo Desert
KwaZulu Natal	The Drakensberg Mountains

chapter seven

TRAVEL, HEALTH, & SECURITY

ARRIVAL

There are several different kinds of entry visa, such as for tourism or business. The South African embassy's Web site will have visa application guidelines.

South Africa's three international airports are O. R. Tambo in Johannesburg, King Shaka in Durban, and Cape Town International. The airports are generally modern and efficient and, apart from customs checks, processing should be smooth.

Be sure to read the customs form in advance to establish what you are allowed to bring into the country—certain foodstuffs, drugs, and the like are prohibited. Drug traffickers are severely dealt with and the airport is awash with sniffer dogs, sniffing out everything from food to drugs.

The main forms of intercity travel are air, rail, and road. There are airports in most major cities.

RAIL

Rail is a popular and exciting way to travel, and several large companies offer a convenient, enjoyable service. The Shosholoza Meyl long-distance passenger train links Johannesburg with Cape Town, Durban, Port

Elizabeth, and East London, and is modern, cheap, and comfortable. It travels along the same route as the expensive Blue Train, but costs only a fraction of the price. The Premier Classe train, The Blue Train, Rovos Rail, and Shongololo are all in the luxury bracket, and well worth it if you have the money.

The Gautrain rapid transit system is a safe and modern electric rail service between Pretoria and Johannesburg and its environs.

The suburban Metro trains around Johannesburg and Pretoria are not considered safe, but those in Cape Town and its surroundings are reasonably safe for travelers from Cape Town to Paarl, Stellenbosch, and Simon's Town.

ROAD

South Africa has an efficient and well-developed road infrastructure, and intercity connections are generally world class. National toll roads are usually in a good state of repair; the national roads that aren't tolls are less comfortable, and the roads off the beaten path are an unknown quantity. One of the major routes to the

World Heritage Site of the Drakensberg is in appalling condition, and there is no sign of any plan to improve it. You'll need a 4x4 vehicle to reach many parts of the beautiful mountain range. In many small towns, taxes aren't paid and municipalities don't have the money to maintain the roads, so driving in South Africa can be either a first-world or a third world-experience. Check the condition of the roads before setting off, and ensure you have a vehicle capable of handling all eventualities.

The highways are always busy over long weekends or during peak holiday times. South Africa's Drive Alive campaign is usually evident during these periods to encourage safe driving. The country has a very high mortality rate caused by motor accidents, many the result of drunk driving, or driving without lights. It's best to be super vigilant when tackling long distances, and it is advisable to take several stops along the way to stretch and have a cup of coffee.

IN TOWN
Most South Africans famously travel around in minibus taxis. They're used by both blacks and whites, but

predominantly by black people. Since there is no central depot, like a bus station, commuters have to familiarize themselves with the routes and pick-up points. Foreign visitors are recommended to travel with a friend or colleague at first. These minibuses are an efficient way of getting around the city, although the drivers tend to ignore the rules of the road, often endangering the lives of their passengers.

Other options are traveling on local buses, such as the Rea Vaya bus system in Johannesburg, or the Gautrain, which serves only certain routes between Pretoria, the O. R. Tambo Airport, and Johannesburg. Uber taxis can be ordered online; simply download the app on arrival, and you're good to go. Uber has become a verb in the suburbs, as in "I'll uber to your house." It's the choice for people who want a night out with friends, partying and drinking, but don't want to be caught driving later by the police.

DRIVING

By and large, South Africans follow the rules of the road. The "don'ts" of driving in South Africa are: don't drink and drive; don't use a cell phone without a hands-free kit. Driving while texting or talking on a cell phone attracts a fine of R5,000.

Driving is on the left-hand side of the road. The speed limits range from 25 mph (40 kmph) in villages to 37.5 mph (60 kmph) in urban areas, and anything from 50 to 75 mph (80 to 120 kmph) on the open road or on highways. Watch your speed, because there are punitive speed traps, especially on the national highways. Most traps are electronic these days, and even if you're driving a rented car you'll be liable for those fines. Don't pick up hitchhikers. Drive carefully, and enjoy the scenery.

When filling up at a garage, as a gas station is known locally, it's not self-service. An attendant will fill up the tank, check the tire pressure, oil, water, and so on, and clean your windshield. Just make sure to tell them whether your car takes diesel or gas. A small tip for the service is always appreciated. All cards are accepted for payment at garages.

Drunk Driving
The legal age limit for drinking is eighteen years, but is likely to go up to twenty-one because of the high incidence of fatal accidents caused by drunk driving. While currently alcohol may be served at establishments until 2:00 a.m., this could also change.

The legal alcohol limit is 0.05 g/100 ml (two standard 340 ml beers), and the penalty for breaching this limit is hefty. Traffic police are constantly on the lookout for drunk drivers, and will pull a suspect over for a breathalyser test. There is the possibility that a traffic officer might claim to be hungry and ask for a bit of KFC money—which, if handed over, will let you off the hook. It's advisable to call a taxi if you think you can't guarantee your sobriety.

Car Rental
Most of the major international car rental companies operate in South Africa. There is a pick-up/drop-off area at the major airports where cars can be rented and returned. It's advisable to take out insurance with the rental company and to do a thorough check of the vehicle with the agent before taking it. There's a saying in South Africa —"drive it like it's a hire car," implying that people don't respect rental cars. So when doing the inspection be sure to check that in addition to the usual features there's no damage to the visible undercarriage,

ROAD RAGE

Road rage is increasingly leading to violent crime, with people suffering severe injuries and even death. Some drivers—mostly young white males or black taxi drivers—are inherently aggressive, and take out their aggression on fellow road users. Drivers who speed, force their way between cars, or fail to signal should be ignored: stay behind them. It's never worth getting into an altercation, since you have no idea whether or not the enraged driver is armed—and ordinary implements, such as a car jack, can be used as a weapon. If you are involved in an incident, don't make eye contact; simply raise your hand, say "Sorry," and drive off.

because if such damage is picked up when you return the car you'll be liable for it.

If you're going camping or on safari, make sure your vehicle is fit for that purpose, such as a 4x4 with high clearance for rough country roads. For city and suburban driving an ordinary sedan will do the job. Include a GPS device if you aren't familiar with the routes. Maps are usually outdated, since most people now rely on electronic mapping devices, especially those on cell phones, which are accurate and reliable. Many suburban streets have been closed off to provide security, and the GPS generally picks up on these closures, as well as where speed traps are located. Overall, they're a useful tool, especially with so many street names being changed. There have been almost a thousand place name changes in South Africa since 1994. Most of these were from names that represented or were connected to the country's painful past, for example Verwoerdburg, after H. F. Verwoerd, the architect of apartheid, to Centurion.

WHERE TO STAY

There is something for everyone. Depending on your budget, you can stay in anything from a palatial hotel to a tent. However, a word of warning: don't rely on Internet pictures, which can be misleading. Look for online reviews or ask locals about the place you have in mind. South Africa's cities are large metropolises and every type of opportunist exists, so it's best to know what you're getting into. A general rule in South Africa is "If it sounds too good to be true, it is!"

The best accommodation is world class, and high standards are maintained in the key national tourist areas. There are the top international hotel brands, and there are many boutique hotels that keep people coming back. The Tourism Grading Council of South Africa ensures that South Africa maintains its international competitiveness as a tourist destination. The star rating system, from 1 to 5, provides a reliable guide to quality and service.

HEALTH

The standard of health care in the country ranges from basic state provision in public clinics and hospitals to state-of-the art medicine in expensive private clinics. Access to health care has improved in rural areas, but the infrastructure is poorly maintained, and often personnel aren't available and medication is scarce. South Africa has world-class medical training, but the state hospitals no longer boast their former proud level of care for a variety of reasons, the main one being lack of funding. So, while there's a network of basic medical provision for everyone, for better treatment one has to go private.

It is advisable to include health cover in your travel insurance. Should you need medical treatment in South Africa you will have to pay for it upfront, and then claim it back from your insurer when you return home. Private health care facilities exist in all the main areas, and public provision is available in most places, but the level of care is unpredictable.

There are no mandatory vaccinations for travelers to South Africa. Precautions should be taken, however, if you are going to the malaria belt in the northeast, near the Mozambique border, and travelers are strongly advised to consult their doctor about medication. At the very least, you should use insect repellent, wear sensible clothing, and sleep under mosquito nets in suspect areas.

It's usually unnecessary to boil water for drinking, or to buy bottled water, though this is widely available. The tap water in South African suburbs is safe to drink; if it isn't, then locals will be able to warn you. Most people take drinking water directly from the tap.

Some areas have been affected by drought, where it's necessary to take bottled water with you. And if you're going to be trekking in remote areas where the water source is unknown or unreliable, then by all means take along water supplies or purification tablets.

HAZARDS
Wildlife
In dense bush or in rural areas there may be snakes and scorpions, but if you're vigilant it's unlikely you'll come across them suddenly, and they are unlikely to wait

around for you. However, ask locals what to expect, and they'll be able to advise you.

Some areas have baboons, especially the nature parks, and you should be on your guard around them. While they might be entertaining or look cute, they are a menace, and can be dangerous. Always observe them from a distance, preferably from behind a window, and under no circumstances approach them. If you come across them, exercise caution. Dominant males have enormous teeth and will attack, especially if the troop has babies.

Generally, if baboons approach people or buildings they're looking for food. Despite warnings not to feed them, some people do, and this often has disastrous results for the baboons, who quickly associate humans with food and are frequently killed because they raid homes. Keep windows and doors locked—they are smart, and can open doors and even refrigerators!

Sun
Nothing beats spending a day in the glorious sunshine, but be warned: the South African sun is very strong. Always wear sunscreen and protective clothing if necessary. Beet-colored visitors who haven't understood this are a common sight at the beaches.

HIV/AIDS
As we have seen, South Africa has a very high incidence of HIV/AIDS, and care should be taken to protect oneself against transmission. (See page 99.)

SAFETY
Violent crime features prominently in South African life, where about fifty murders take place daily. Most

criminal activity occurs in the poorer areas and is usually gang or drug-related, and few visitors are likely to come across it. In the affluent areas people tend to live in gated communities, or houses with high fences and security. Despite the lurid headlines about murder and rape, it is certainly possible to enjoy a holiday in South Africa without coming into contact with the dangerous elements of society.

Safety Tips

Since most South Africans are friendly, it's difficult not to be caught up in the camaraderie and let your guard down. However, you need to bear in mind that some people, no matter how they present themselves to you, may have ulterior motives. The number one rule in terms of personal safety is to be sensible and trust your instincts. Don't go to areas you're not familiar with unless you're with someone you know and trust. Don't trust strangers who try to encourage you to go with them, and don't travel or walk around alone in the dark. If you're feeling unsure, position yourself in a well-lit area where you can ask other people for help, or where you can call for help. Don't ever go with someone if you don't feel comfortable with them.

As fast as you put down your purse or your laptop is as fast as it can be stolen. In a restaurant or sidewalk café, always try to sit at an interior table, since tables on the periphery are usually the ones targeted by thieves who can grab your valuables and run. If you hang your purse on the back of your chair, a couple of people may work in tandem to remove it. If you go to the restroom while you're at a restaurant, take your belongings with you, or they won't be there when you return.

Most shopping centers or village streets have security guards. If you approach them for assistance, don't be surprised if they don't help you. Many are foreigners, who won't understand you, and are merely a presence to ward off petty criminals. If you need help, head into one of the stores or restaurants and ask the manager to call the police—who may or may not arrive.

The South African Police Service is understaffed, overworked, and under-resourced. If they have a patrol car in a small town, it may not be working, or may already be out on a call. The police are unlikely to bother with minor incidents; they are more likely

to arrive for serious offenses such as rape or a carjacking. If you should fall victim to a crime, it's best to go to the local police station yourself and report it there, where you will be given a case number so that you can make the necessary

insurance claim. That is probably the sum extent of police cooperation in petty crimes. It is unheard of that they investigate the theft of a cell phone or jewelry. Major crimes take precedence.

Because the police are overstretched in every way, treat them with respect and calmly. The saying "honey gets the money" means that you're more likely to get a favorable and helpful response if you're measured and respectful. Already stressed policemen are unlikely to react sympathetically to a hysterical victim.

You will see warning notices posted in some areas where crime frequently takes place. Take heed of these—they're there to protect you. Areas that may not have these signs but still require vigilance are secluded beaches and veld areas.

Personal Safety

The number for general emergencies is 10111. If you are traveling, it's wise to let someone know where you're going in advance. Explore unknown areas in groups, and stick to busy, well-lit areas. If you are traveling with children be particularly watchful, as there have been cases of abduction. Always accompany them into a public toilet.

Don't display valuables such as cash, credit cards, traveler's checks, cell phones, jewelry, or cameras in public. Don't carry more cash than you need, and don't leave valuable possessions in a cart or stroller.

In a hotel, don't leave your luggage unattended. Store valuables in the safe deposit box. Keep your room locked, when you are in it as well as out of it, and if someone knocks on the door, check who is there before opening it. Hand your keys in when you go out, rather than carrying them with you.

If you are driving, plan your route in advance and let someone know your plans. Keep car doors locked and windows closed at all times, particularly in towns. Be extra cautious when driving alone, especially at night. Be sure to park in well-lit areas at night, and avoid stopping at remote places (or at least be cautious, day or night). Don't leave valuables unattended in the vehicle; rather place them in the trunk. Don't give lifts to strangers.

Safety at the ATM

ATM fraud is a major problem. Be alert at all times, and if you see anything suspicious abandon your transaction and leave. Don't accept help from a stranger. If an ATM is poorly lit or appears to be damaged, leave and find another one, preferably inside a bank. Never give your PIN to anyone. Don't count your money in public.

chapter eight

BUSINESS BRIEFING

South Africa's economy is one of the strongest and most mature in Africa. However, in recent years it has been compromised by political manipulation and the attempted "capture" of key state institutions, such as the Treasury, the South African Reserve Bank, and the courts, by government officials, some of whom are in cahoots with powerful foreign business interests. In 2017, after the dismissal of the respected finance minister, the Rand fell and rating agencies Standard & Poor's and Fitch downgraded South Africa's credit rating, while Moody's placed it under review.

South Africa is referred to as a "developing" country, and the unreliability of electricity and water supplies still hampers growth by interrupting production and discouraging investment. In spite of these failings and the dim economic outlook, it continues to have a strong manufacturing sector that is taking advantage of the weak Rand to export goods.

As we have seen, the South African economy operates on two levels—the formal and the informal. There is a big divide between the two. The formal economy is where business is above board and transparent. It adheres to the law, registering businesses and paying taxes, and the informal one does not. With an unemployment rate hovering at around 40 percent, the informal or street economy is huge, despite misleading official statistics—ranging from the level of people at traffic lights wanting to wash your windshield to home mechanics who service vehicles from their front yards in the townships.

HOW BUSINESS IS DONE IN SOUTH AFRICA
The Old School Tie
In business circles there are certain networks that work together to support each other. This is evident in the Old School Tie brigade of men (and increasingly women) who went to the same school or university, and it's evident in the role played by tribal allegiance. Nepotism has become increasingly conspicuous in black business appointments, and even though Broad Based Black Employment Equity exists to regulate business (see below), personal contacts are strong factors in determining who does business with whom, and to whom contracts are awarded.

Corruption
From the boardrooms in Sandton to the hallowed halls of parliament and the back streets of Khayelitsha

township, corruption is rife. Business often takes place at the whim of someone in a position of power, whether it's the procurement clerk in a parastatal company or a political crony. Bribes are still paid in cash or kind, in spite of checks and balances to prevent these forms of corruption.

When establishing a business in South Africa it is advisable to employ one of the top financial consultants, such as KPMG or Pricewaterhouse Coopers, to advise you on local laws and business practices.

South Africa has passed the Financial Intelligence Centre Act, which in effect has empowered banks and property brokers, among others, to report suspect sources of money. It's not as effective as the government would like, and much dirty business goes on that escapes FICA's notice. There has only been one high-profile case of the banks refusing to do business with a prominent family allegedly attempting to capture state departments for its own benefit. Fraud is a significant issue for companies experiencing "white-collar crime." Private investigation firms have their hands full investigating corporate crimes.

Crimes of any nature, including fraud, can be reported anonymously to the Crime Line on toll-free number 0800 847 633.

AFFIRMATIVE ACTION

The government has passed two major pieces of legislation to help address the problem of social and economic inequality in South Africa: the Preferential Procurement Policy Framework Act, and the Broad-Based Economic Empowerment Act.

Preferential Procurement

The Preferential Procurement Policy Framework Act, 2000 (PP) concerns the proper management of public moneys and aims to redress the socio-economic imbalances of the past by awarding government work to historically disadvantaged individuals (HDI).

It set in place a policy where bids (tenders) are awarded on a points system where preference is given to HDI South African citizens, rather than being awarded solely on compliance with the specification or cost. An HDI can score points only if he or she is involved in the day to-day running of the business.

While the policy's aims are laudable, it is open to abuse in a business culture of patronage.

Black Economic Empowerment

The Black Economic Empowerment Act of 2003 (BEE) set out to redress the economic injustices of apartheid and to promote greater economic participation by black people. However, it didn't result in the kind of transformation that the government had hoped for. In fact, it was severely criticized for helping only a few politically well-connected individuals, instead of uplifting the great majority of poor people. Additionally, some black companies acted as fronts for white companies—being the "black face" demanded by government dealings and contracts—in return for a share of the profits.

In 2007 a new code of affirmative action was introduced: Broad-Based Black Economic Empowerment (BBBEE). In essence, companies wishing to do business with the government have to obtain a BEE certificate from an accredited BEE rating agency based on a scorecard for that specific industry. This certificate determines the number of "empowerment" points, which will be given to the bidder when awarding a bid.

This legislation, demanding that in particular categories white businesspeople have to share a certain percentage of their business with a black partner, has had a severe impact on their morale and drive. Many white South Africans have closed their businesses, or downsized, or broken up their company into smaller units to fall outside the parameters of the legislation. Some have emigrated to escape what they perceive to be punitive laws against white people doing business in South Africa.

BUSINESS ETIQUETTE
Setting up Meetings
South African businesspeople are generally accessible and meetings can be arranged by a phone call. Introductions aren't normally required, although a personal contact may secure a meeting more readily than calling the company yourself.

Meetings can be held in a boardroom, a hotel, a coffee shop, or with an *induna* (tribal leader) under a tree in a village. It's not so much about where the meeting is held, as about the respect that you bring to it. Wherever the meeting is held, South African businesspeople expect it to be on time. If you are running late, let them know.

Dress
There really isn't a set dress code for business; it depends on the sector you're working in. Most large legal and financial companies demand greater formality—suits for men and professional-level dresses

or trouser suits for women. However, there are small to medium- sized companies that are more relaxed about business dress and probably the only no-no is arriving at work in beach clothes—shorts and skimpy tops for women aren't acceptable. Friday is usually Casual Day across the country, when you can wear comfortable leisurewear. If any of the national teams are playing an international match on the weekend, South Africans usually wear their national team's sports shirt to work. On National Heritage Day it's acceptable to wear your national dress to work.

Greetings

Err on the side of formality when greeting South Africans of any color. Always address them as Mr., Mrs., or Miss. If they feel comfortable with you, they will invite you to call them by their first name. Until they do so, continue to address them formally.

Many black South African names are difficult to pronounce, but persevere—after all, we all appreciate it when someone goes to the trouble of learning our name. If you convene the meeting, you can organize name tags, so that everyone can familiarize themselves with each other's names.

Even if you don't get the African handshake down pat, don't withdraw your hand too soon from the handshake—a lingering grasp tells the other person that you're interested in getting to know them.

MEETINGS

At the meeting don't get straight down to business. Spend a little time on pleasantries to break the ice.

Most meetings take place in ordinary venues such as a company boardroom, with straightforward agendas and standard negotiating practices. However, a lot of business is still conducted in social settings—it might be a breakfast meeting, a power lunch, a round of golf, or a dinner engagement.

The *bosberaad* (bush conference) is a meeting held away from the office, either to enhance a negotiation or to improve company performance. It usually takes place in a game or nature reserve, and although it will have a structured agenda it is usually fairly informal. *Bosberade* (plural) can be an opportunity to break the ice between new employees, a brainstorming session, or a serious strategy conference. They can be formal or informal, so take your cue from the agenda.

PRESENTATIONS

The best approach when making a pitch to South Africans is to be straightforward but not boring. South Africans aren't impressed by PowerPoint presentations, but will respond to humor and anecdotes. While you're talking, people may well be busy on their smartphones or with coffee cups. Don't take this personally; it doesn't show lack of interest. Always leave time for questions and answers at the end of your presentation.

NEGOTIATIONS AND CONTRACTS

There's no template for negotiations, but generally South Africans are to-the-point and pleasant. In some negotiations the decision makers will be present, and in others they will send colleagues to negotiate and report back. Try to ascertain in advance who will be there, so that you can ensure that the person you need to talk to is in fact going to be at the meeting.

Legislation governing business in South Africa is fairly complex, so it's advisable to take on a South African consultant or partner who will be present during negotiations, the drawing up of contracts, and at follow-up sessions. As we have seen, government departments must adhere to strict guidelines and policies when procuring goods and services.

Contract law in South Africa is a modernized version of the Roman–Dutch law of contract. It provides the legally binding framework for transactions. Contracts can be oral or written, with the exception of property transactions, suretyships, credit agreements, marriage contracts, and executionary donations, which have to be in writing and signed by the parties. Contracts may be drawn up directly by the parties concerned, but if you're unsure of the implications of the fine print it is advisable to employ a lawyer. The terms should specify the legal remedy in the event of a dispute.

BUSINESS ENTERTAINMENT

Businesses in South Africa aren't shy about spending money on promotions and product launches, and these can range from a day in the Winelands to a week in the bushveld, with all creature comforts thrown in. Once a contract has been concluded, it is common courtesy to celebrate with dinner at a fine restaurant. Conversely, if you entertain clients or customers, you are of course expected to foot the bill.

MANAGING DISAGREEMENT

Parties can choose to resolve disputes by arbitration, and thus include an arbitration clause in their contract, or they can choose to rely on the courts to handle disputes, and a jurisdiction clause states that they have agreed to the courts of a named country taking jurisdiction over any disputes that may arise. South African courts are fair and impartial. Disputes between businesses are dealt with in the magistrates' courts, high courts, or the Supreme Court, depending on the value attached to the dispute.

South Africa's Commission for Conciliation, Mediation and Arbitration (CCMA) deals with disputes between employees and employers within companies. While this is the legal route, it's always better to try to deal with disagreements on a human level first. Sometimes disputes are a case of misunderstanding, and a conversation or discussion where all the parties have a chance to give their side of the story can result in a resolution. However, one should be aware of cultural sensitivities or different ways of dealing with problems. In cases of serious transgressions the legal route may be the only option.

TRADE UNIONS AND BARGAINING COUNCILS

South Africa has a sophisticated trade union movement that goes back to the early twentieth century. In 2016, 3.11 million workers were members of a trade union, representing 25.3 percent of the formal work force.

Additionally, Bargaining Councils determine each sector's terms and conditions of operation. Legislation differs between sectors, so it is wise to get an expert to advise you on the sector in which you intend to operate. There has been much criticism of the Bargaining Councils, with SMEs stating that they're kept back by laws made by the big conglomerates. Nevertheless, business is done and can be done, and it will take a couple of hours for an expert to bring you up to speed on the sector you intend to enter.

There are Web sites that can advise you on doing business in South Africa and these are provided in the recommended section at the end of this guide.

WOMEN IN BUSINESS

The role of women in business in South Africa has changed remarkably since 1994, with many more women participating in economic life. Approximately 72 percent of micro-enterprises and 40 percent of SMEs in South Africa are owned by women; however, only 28 percent of the top decision-making roles in SA business are filled by women. According to the 2010 Census figures, an

estimated 51 percent of women in the country actively contribute to South Africa's GDP. South African women earn less than men, largely because they are predominantly employed in informal sectors and have little influence in decision making.

chapter nine

COMMUNICATING

LANGUAGE

The country's eleven official languages are Afrikaans, English, isiNdebele, Sepedi, Sesotho, Setswana, SiSwati, Tshivenda, isiXhosa, Xitsonga, and isiZulu. In addition to these are the languages spoken by indigenous people, such as the Nama in the northern Cape, and immigrants, who speak Gujarati, Hindi, Mandarin, Cantonese, French, Portuguese, German, Greek, and Italian. Whether people are speaking isiNdebele, SiSwati, or English, South Africans are a pretty vocal lot and aren't shy about raising their voices, often talking to each other across the street, or from street corner to street corner.

Inevitably, the languages influence each other and various South African creoles have developed. South African English has many words and phrases taken from isiZulu and Afrikaans, and African language speakers often use English and Afrikaans expressions. "Tsotsitaal," also known as *iscamtho*, developed in the cities and townships as a means of communication between the different black language groups. It is a dynamic language that grows daily as new words and phrases are added. Fanagalo is a pidgin that developed to facilitate communication between the white supervisors and black laborers during the colonial and apartheid eras. It's a simplified version of isiZulu and isiXhosa that incorporates English, Afrikaans, Dutch, and Portuguese.

One of the most distinctive dialects is the Afrikaans spoken by the Coloureds of the Western Cape, called *Kaaps*. This vibrant vernacular, peppered with exclamations and sayings taken from all the country's official languages and colorful expletives, is often accompanied by expressive body movements. It is energetic, eloquent, and attractive to most who hear it.

Formal Language Learning

In Grades 1 and 2 it is compulsory for schoolchildren to study in one of the approved languages, and from Grade 3 onward they must learn at least one additional approved language. Black South Africans are pretty multilingual, usually speaking English, a smattering of Afrikaans, and two or more African languages. Young white South Africans (who study in English- or Afrikaans-language schools) usually learn a black language at school, and older white people are starting to show an interest in learning an African language.

BODY LANGUAGE

In South Africa body language affects how people view each other and how they assess status. A well-dressed man with a firm handshake is generally considered to be a person with power, while a man dressed casually with poor posture and a weak handshake is the stereotypical inferior. Non-verbal signals vary according to place, and to a person's age. In urban areas, eye contact is expected, but in rural areas it is considered rude to meet the gaze of a superior. Often black employees who don't make eye contact are thought to be lying or to have something to hide by white or Western interlocutors, when in fact they are being respectful.

Some South Africans are physically expressive and gesticulate; others are restrained or demure. Gestures that should be avoided are pointing a finger at someone, standing too close while speaking to someone (among whites), and keeping your hands in your pockets or on your hips while speaking to people.

Laborers waiting at busy intersections to be offered piece work indicate their willingness by raising a fore-finger, meaning they're looking for a job for the day.

TWELFTH OFFICIAL LANGUAGE— TAXI HAND SIGNALS

Hand signals to passing taxis are the silent language of South African commuters. They use ingenious hand and finger combinations to indicate their destination, and if the taxi is going that way he will pull over and stop, usually without any warning to motorists behind him.

An upraised index finger tells the driver that you're heading for town. Other gestures are more elaborate. Some are tied to significant places or events. A hand turned palm-side up with fingers grasping an invisible fruit indicates that the destination is Orange Farm. The universal train station route is indicated by the "choo-choo" train-wheel arm movement. To get a ride to the Chris Hani Baragwanath Hospital, which has a history of treating victims of gun violence, commuters show the gun hand signal. Commuters residing near the Leeuwkop Prison gesture with a handcuffed hands sign.

The most forceful body language is used by irate motorists, who will "flip the bird" regularly to indicate that they're unimpressed by your road manners.

CONVERSATION

English is the lingua franca, but South African English is peppered with words taken from all the local cultures. There are South Africanisms, and there are Kasi or Tsotsitaal expressions—usually Afrikaans words that have been incorporated into Bantu languages and assimilated into daily conversation. Kasi, a shortening of the Afrikaans word *lokasie*, refers to the townships, also known as locations, and Tsotsitaal refers to language that appeared in Sophiatown in the 1940s and 1950s that was mainly spoken by the criminal element, using words that were deliberately oblique to obscure their actual meaning and maintain secrecy. In Soweto, 500,000 youth now use Tsotsitaal as one of their daily languages.

TSOTSITAAL

Babalaz: a hangover
Ma-gents: guys
Moja: good
Pinkies: R50
Popa: to hit the jackpot, to get lucky
Ringa: to talk
Shesha: hurry
Timer: an elderly man or father, as in old timer
Transi: a car
Vaya: move

SOME SOUTH AFRICANISMS

Ag: Used to express resignation or irritation, as in: "Ag no man! Why did you do that?" Pronounced as in German "*ach*"

Boet/bru: A term of affection, from the Afrikaans for "brother"

Eish: Used to express surprise, wonder, frustration or outrage

Fundi: Expert. From Zulu *umfundisi*, "teacher"

Gogo: Grandmother or elderly woman

Howzit: A traditional South African greeting that translates roughly as "How are you?," "How are things?", or simply "Hello"

Jawelnofine/ja-nee: Literally, "yes, well, no, fine," similar to the rhetorical "How about that?"

Lekker: Great, good, or tasty

Mzansi: Zulu for "south," but used for for South Africa as a whole

Now-now: Shortly, in a bit

Pasop: "beware" or "watch out"

Shame!: Broadly denotes everything from cuteness to sympathy. As in "Ag, shame!"

Skebenga/skelm: Gangster, criminal

Spaza: Informal township shop

Toyi-toyi: A high-stepping, chanting protest dance

Voetsek: Go away! Scram!

Yebo: Yes. Used to show agreement or approval

HUMOR

Humor has always been a way for South Africans to temper the tension of living in a political powder keg. South Africans love a good joke, and are able to laugh at themselves. Van der Merwe jokes, in which the eponymous simple-minded farmer is the butt of the joke, are on the wane but still crack a laugh, while Gatiep and Meraai (two old mountain tramps) jokes are usually hilarious and slightly off-color. Satire is a strong art form and satirists such as Pieter-Dirk Uys, Nataniel, and Trevor Noah are well known. South Africa has regular satirical comedy shows, which help people to laugh at themselves.

SWEARING
The F-word abounds in youth culture, and most South Africans are very relaxed about swearing—for many it's a normal part of conversation. However, in polite company it is not acceptable to swear, and many people find it offensive. Some men will happily use expletives in adult male company, but tone their language down when women and children are present. The Cape Coloureds, in particular, swear a great deal in everyday speech and have turns of phrase that it is impossible not to laugh at. Profanity and innuendo are an intrinsic part of their repartee. Indeed, swearing is almost a form of expression, not an intention to insult or offend.

THE MEDIA
Most South African homes have radios. Radio is the main source of music, news, and information for the majority of South Africans. In addition to the state broadcaster there are local commercial radio stations that keep most migrant black workers in touch with their villages' goings on.

Although media freedom is guaranteed under the Constitution, in recent years there have been increasing attempts to curtail it. Legislation—the Protection of State Information, or Secrecy Bill, as it is known—was passed in 2013 to protect both sensitive state information and information about private citizens, such as marriage certificates and business registrations. This ultimately gave the minister of information control of the classification of information. Opponents of the law maintain that whistle-blowers will be compromised, and that state interests are given preference over transparency and freedom of expression. State-run television is administered by ANC die-hards, and blatant preference is given to ANC-related activities.

The state broadcaster is the South African Broadcasting Corporation. The main SABC channels, SABC 1, 2, and 3, are the main source of television entertainment for most South Africans, and provide content in the mother tongue of most of the eleven official languages, while Dstv is the pay channel, with international news brands such as CNN and BBC and more entertainment channels.

In terms of print media, every major city has at least two daily newspapers, and there are many local weeklies. Most black and white households read daily newspapers, either in print or online, and the Sunday editions. Popular print and online newspapers are *The Sowetan*, *The Mail & Guardian*, *The Star*, and online *The Daily Maverick*. Most news is accessed online these days, since most South Africans have cell phones. Many international magazines are available, as well as an assortment of local publications, but the magazine market has dropped significantly with the rise of the Internet.

TELEPHONES

For many years the state-owned Telkom was the sole landline service provider, but with the advent of fiber optic cable, new players have come into the market, such as Neotel and Vumatel. Compared to the rest of the world, the rates are still not competitive, but each provider offers different rates, so it's always best to compare pricing.

Cell Phone Culture

It's almost impossible be out and about and not come across people talking on their cell phones. Even the hallowed bastion of propriety, the country club, has taken down the "No cell phone" signs, realizing that everyone simply has to be connected. However, banks don't allow the use of cell phones or the wearing of crash helmets on the premises, to avoid collusion between criminals in and outside the bank.

Cell phone vendors can be found on every street corner and there are four major service providers, namely Vodacom, MTN, Cell C, and Telkom Mobile. There are 80 million active cell phone connections in South Africa, meaning that the average South African has 1.5 cell phone SIM cards activated. Because rates vary between service providers, it makes sense to switch networks as and when the need arises. However, the cost of cell phone services, both calls and data, is excessively high in comparison with the rest of the world. It's best to shop around for the best deal.

MAIL

In the past the Post Office was a reliable institution that offered good, fast service. However its service declined dramatically in the early 2000s. Although it is still state-owned, it is now run by an entrepreneur and the service has improved, especially in the metros, with changes taking a little longer to reach rural areas. Mail will arrive, but a courier company is preferable for the delivery of important or urgent documents.

CONCLUSION

South Africa is a nation in transition. With its evolving mix of cultures and identities, it is a difficult but fascinating society to fathom. It has been called the "laboratory of mankind," a place where people from all the nations of the world coexist. It's where you'll encounter black evangelists worshiping in city towers, Hindus throwing offerings into the rivers, cable car rides to the top of the mountain, and horse riders on the wild unspoiled beaches.

If you've visited South Africa, you are not likely ever to forget the smell of Highveld thunderstorms, the scent of a wood fire, a lion's grunt carried across the stillness of the bushveld, the shriek of the hadedas birds in the suburbs, the deep orange sunsets in the interior, or the violet moods of the oceans.

South Africans might sometimes come across as loud, and even aggressive, but they're basically friendly and hospitable. Their warmth, directness, openness, and vitality are what make them likeable and your visit all the more memorable.

Further Reading

Berger, Lee. *Almost Human: The Astonishing Tale of* Homo naledi. Cape Town:. Jonathan Ball Publishers, 2017.

Callinicos, Luli. *The World that Made Mandela.* Gauteng: Real African Publishers, 2001.

Kessler, S. *The Black Concentration Camps of the Anglo Boer War 1899–1902.* Bloemfontein: War Museum of the Boer Republics, 2012.

Krog, A. *Country of My Skull: Guilt, sorrow, and the limits of forgiveness in the New South Africa.* New York: Broadway Books, 2000.

Mandela, Nelson. *Long Walk to Freedom.* London: Abacus, 1995.

Mashaba, H. *Capitalist Crusader.* Johannesburg: BookStorm, 2015.

Molamu, L. *Tsotsitaal: A Dictionary of the Language of Sophiatown.* Pretoria: Unisa Press, 2003.

Ndebele, N.S, *Fine Lines from the Box: further thoughts about our country.* Cape Town: Umuzi, 2007.

Ndebele, N.S. *Rediscovery of the Ordinary.* Scottsville, SA: UKZN Press, 2006.

Reitz, D. *Commando: A Boer Journal of the Boer War.* Cape Town: Jonathan Ball Publishers, 1998.

Welsh, F. *A History of South Africa.* London: Harper Collins, 2000.

Wilson, F. *Dinosaurs, Diamonds & Democracy: A Short, Short History of South Africa.* Cape Town: Umuzi, 2017.

Useful Web Sites

www.brandsouthafrica.com (official custodian of South Africa's national brand)

www.gov.za (government departments)

www.dailymaverick.co.za (daily online newspaper)

www.news24.com/SouthAfrica (online newspaper)

www.mg.co.za (*Mail&Guardian* on-line weekly newspaper)

www.sahistory.org.za (history site)

www.southafrica.net (everything you need to know on SA)

www.wheretostay.co.za (accommodation guide)

Index

Acknowledgments

With special thanks to my husband, Mark Morris, for his unfailing support; to David Holt-Biddle for a framework on which to build; and to Ufrieda Ho for passing it forward.